AKASHA UNLEASHED

The Missing Manual to You

Debbra Lupien

Lupien Limited
CRESCO, PENNSYLVANIA

Lupien Limited
7949 Route 191
Cresco, PA 18326
AkashaUnleashed.com

Book Layout © 2017 BookDesignTemplates.com
Copy editing by Stephanie Gunning
Cover design by Gus Yoo

Akasha Unleashed/ Debbra Lupien. -- 1st ed.

Library of Congress Control Number: 2017915411

ISBN 978-0-9994880-1-0

DEDICATION

To David, my partner and steadfast rock, you believed in and supported me through all the highs and lows. No matter how wacky my ideas may have seemed, no matter what anyone else said, you were always on board, cheering me on.

In loving memory of Grandma "Sally," who made the unbearable bearable and without whom I wouldn't have made it this far.

CONTENTS

NOTE

Throughout this book, the terms *Creator, Creator of all that is, God, Source,* and *the Universe* will be used to indicate a divine higher power. Do not get distracted by these titles. Please feel free to substitute whatever term is comfortable for you.

INTRODUCTION

Every appliance comes with a manual. When you buy a refrigerator, a washing machine, or a car, it comes with an owner's manual. When something goes wrong, you simply consult the instructions, fix the device if you can, or bring in an expert.

When you think about it, we human beings are far more complex than a car or a refrigerator. How wonderful would it be if there was a manual we could consult when we need help?

Well, I'm here to tell you that there is a manual you can consult. It's a spiritual tool located in the fifth dimension (a place outside time and space) called the Akashic Records. What's more, each of us has a unique archive that's curated and maintained by our own personal team of masters, teachers, angels, and spirit guides—energetic beings who reside in the fifth dimension that act as liaisons between humans and God. Their job is to facilitate our journey to higher consciousness in any way they can without violating our freedom of choice. The information they share comes from the Creator, therefore it is always true. Your Akashic Records are dedicated solely to helping you on your journey to higher consciousness.

Yes, your Akashic Records are truly the missing manual to you.

What Are Your Akashic Records?

Your Akashic Records are a gift from your Creator—your birthright—intended to be used to help you navigate the often complex and confusing journey of life.

If you're like me, upon hearing this for the first time, you are probably wondering, *Why in the heck didn't somebody tell me this sooner? Why didn't they teach us this stuff in grammar school?*

The answer to these questions is that your parents and teachers didn't know. Until recently, the energetic frequency of humankind (except for a small number of individuals) wasn't high enough to gain access to the Akashic Records.

All energy has a frequency, which is the speed at which it vibrates. As humans, our journey is about reaching higher consciousness. Our vibrational frequency rises as we gain more awareness of ourselves and the universe. Some souls on Earth today have a much higher frequency than others. That is a testament to the spiritual work they have done. Those with lower frequencies are simply not as far along in their soul journeys.

Neither high nor low frequency is better than the other. Wherever you are on your journey to higher consciousness is perfect for you. There is no judgment in the records. A person's soul journey can never be wrong.

Edgar Cayce, known to his contemporaries as the Sleeping Prophet, gained access to the Akashic Records in the early 1900s while in a trance state. The disparity between his waking energy and the energy of the records at that time was still so broad that being in a trance state was the only way he could gain entry. While in trance, he would speak aloud, reporting on what he perceived, and someone else carefully recorded every detail he said, then relayed it to Cayce's clients and preserved the transcriptions for historical purposes. Edgar would come out of his trances with no memory of what had transpired.

Cayce's transmissions helped a great many people, including many with serious health issues. The accuracy of his information has been validated extensively and may still be studied today through his foundation, the Association for Research and Enlightenment (see Resources), and in books.

During the last century, enough people energetically shifted that more of us can now gain access to the Akashic Records—and do so during a waking state. As our collective consciousness has evolved, the records have become so accessible that you need only perform a quick Google search to locate hundreds, if not thousands, of individuals, like me, who regularly access them.

Your Akashic Records contain every minute detail of your soul's journey since you were created. This includes details from every lifetime you have lived. If you are like most people, you have lived many lifetimes before this one.

Why Is Having Access to the Records Important?

There are two main reasons why we would want to access our Akashic Records. First, our souls have amassed a great deal of wisdom through their past-life experiences. Opening the door to your records allows you to tap into this resource to help you understand yourself better. Accessing this wisdom can super charge your life in the very best possible way.

Second, everyone carries karmic "baggage" from their past lives. Karma is the law of cause and effect that rules the universe. And it doesn't end when we die in one life. It follows us to the next, and from lifetime to lifetime, if we do not re-solve it. Karma typically shows up in our lives in the form of repeating patterns.

Although you may not consciously be aware of your karma yet, this doesn't change the fact that it's impacting you. Unrecognized karmic patterns may mean that you struggle and strain far more than you must.

Why would you do this if you could simply re-move the obstacle, drop the karmic baggage, and travel lighter on your life's journey?

In your Akashic Records, there are stories from previous lives that can explain aspects of the pat-terns you're currently experiencing. Patterns from choices made in our past lives repeat until we un-lock the mystery of those choices and consciously release them. Once you understand the choice that served as the catalyst for a given present-day challenge to occur, you can release the karma re-lated to the choice and move forward, making new, more empowered choices. This may feel like cutting loose a giant anvil to which you've been shackled.

You can either learn to read your own Akashic Records or you can have someone else with the ability read them for you and report back, like Ed-gar Cayce did for his clients.

Who Needs a Blueprint?

Your personal Akashic Records are a kind of energetic blueprint to your soul's essence. It is a schematic, so to speak, showing how your soul is "wired." Your personal records explain everything: your soul characteristics, specialties, gifts, life lessons, and so on, and how to use them for empowerment so that you can have more success, happiness, and peace.

Reading the Akashic Records (or having someone read them for you) is like being given the keys to a secret treasure chamber. The door was there all along, you just needed to unlock it.

And can I tell you a secret I've discovered?

You are the hidden treasure! You're what you've been searching for. The authentic you. The truth of who you are—at soul level.

Known as *The Book of Life* in biblical texts, your Akashic Records are a vehicle of opportunity that will allow you to create a new, more phenomenal life. Imagine you've been driving a car with a flat tire all your life. The ride was bumpy and uncomfortable. You didn't have a spare, so you just kept going, hoping things would magically get better. They didn't. But they can!

Now that you know how to get powerful soul insights, you have the option of consulting your manual, fixing the "flat tire," and getting back on your road. You can be like a finely tuned Ferrari speeding down the highway. Just imagine how wonderful it will feel to have such power coursing through your being and knowing what to do with it.

Are you ready to fix that "flat"?

I communicate with my Akashic guides through meditation and *channeling*. Channeling is a form of communication with nonphysical intelligence. For purposes of my work in reading the Akashic Records, my soul consciousness is receiving and translating messages from another dimension. However, I always maintain complete control over my body.

This is a message about the human experience my guides shared during one meditation.

A very long time ago, before each of you inhabited your current body, you made choices about the direction your new lives would take. You had grand plans about all that you would accomplish. This is not at all unusual for a soul. From the vantage point on this side of the veil, things look very different. But once you step into the physical dimension, the law of gravity becomes a factor and it can feel like trying to run in water. The drag on your body slows you down, making you work harder and with more focus than you expected before you inhabited the body. Sometimes this will cause you to give up and abandon your plans, or perhaps choose to take a different, easier path. Perfectly understandable. However, if you can learn to stop fighting the "water," moving slowly and deliberately, you will discover that the water will actually help you move more fluidly and with greater power as it helps you channel your efforts more effectively. Do you see?

Move with the water rather than against it. Yes, you will move slower than you did in the fifth dimension, but in the end, you will still arrive at your destination—the completion of this life cycle or reaching a certain milestone in it—and you will be energized by your journey rather than depleted. When you learn to stop flailing about, and become one with your environment, you will find that even the friction of gravity feels less restraining.

CHAPTER ONE

AKASHIC RECORDS EXPLAINED

The Akashic Records are a gift from the Creator—your birthright.

Your Birthright

Every soul, at the moment of creation, receives its own Akashic archive. Within your personal archive are records documenting your soul's entire existence, which is vast.

The word *akasha* is Sanskrit for "ether" or "sky." You might think of the records in their totality as a library or gigantic database stored on a massive hard drive—with storage in the fifth dimension being energetic.

Can you wrap your mind around how incredibly important you must be to merit such an archive?

Your personal archive, or user's manual, as I like to call it, contains every detail about how your soul is "wired." Consider this wiring your "software." A description of your unique combination of gifts, specialties, and more is contained in this archive. Imagine that it resembles a gigantic flow chart or diagram of electrical circuits with your name emblazoned at the top.

This archive is intended to be an empowerment tool to aid you on your journey towards higher consciousness—once you discover its existence. Legend has it that we can only discover the Akashic Records when we're ready to avail ourselves of their wisdom.

Congratulations! For you, that day has now arrived!

Until you become well acquainted with this valuable tool, you won't be able to take full advantage of it. That's the purpose for this book: to restore your knowledge of your birthright so that you can use it to have, do, or be anything you would like. With this knowledge, you can create an incredible, empowered life—one that is more delicious than you have yet realized.

At last! You've discovered the "missing manual" to you.

My Mission

Since originally reading my own Akashic Records, I've gone through a tremendous transformation. To call it life changing is not an exaggeration. More about that later. Now I'm on a mission to spread the word about the Akashic Records and share this incredible tool of transformation and empowerment with as many people as possible.

In addition to the juicy details mentioned above, your archive contains a record of *all* your life experiences. Every. Single. Lifetime.

You might wonder, *Why is that important?* Because, within these details can be found answers to explain why you are who you are and exactly where you are, at this time in your soul's development. And this is only a small portion of the information your records hold.

Karmic Baggage

We all carry karmic baggage from past lives. This karma shows up as repeating patterns in our present-day lives. These patterns continue until we at last understand the root cause. Your archive holds the answer to this and all questions you could possibly have about your soul.

Understanding the negative choices you made in a previous incarnation or earlier in life, and the consequences of those choices that created a pattern, allows you to energetically release it, as if you were taking out the trash, thus setting you free to move forward.

If you're not conscious of the reasons behind the repeating patterns in your life, how can you be expected to resolve them and move on? And how could you uncover the roots of a pattern in a previous incarnation without a tool like the records? Even with the help of a skilled therapist, it's unlikely you would get to the root cause.

I speak from experience, and I had an excellent therapist.

Self, Meet Soul

In my opinion, the nature of your *divine gift* is the most important nugget of information contained in your Akashic Records.

And what is a divine gift? Simply put, it's an area of expertise. The way your soul is wired to function optimally. Often the talents that are as easy as breathing (for you) to exercise are a part of your gift. However, because these characteristics and abilities come so easily, it's natural to take them for granted, or worse, to consider them a shortcoming. (You'd probably be amazed at how often that happens.) You may be unaware that others do not possess your special abilities because they are your normal.

It is common not to understand how vitally important and special our divine gifts are, and therefore how valuable we are. If you don't understand the importance of your gift, how can you possibly expect to use it effectively to live a more empowered and consciously aware life? The very purpose of a human, third-dimensional experience is to raise our consciousness.

When I finally discovered my own divine gift, it felt as if at last I had been introduced to myself. I gained a deep understanding of how my soul was wired, empowering me to live with more clarity and purpose. The tag line on my website, "Where self meets soul," encapsulates what I believe the Akashic Records are all about. My soul purpose is introducing other people to their souls.

The Backstory

Early in my career, I worked for a large corporation. While I had an excellent job, and was paid quite well, it was a terrible fit for me. I chafed at the rigid structure and rules that made no sense to my way of thinking. I was mystified that the individuals who did the least work seemed to get the most recognition. I intensely disliked how people were treated like numbers by our employers. It seemed to me that so many decisions were bad and cost the company money, when the intention was, presumably, to make a profit. How did they manage to stay in business?! Imagine how much more money they could have generated if they'd made better decisions?

Similar questions arose over and over again, along with my frustration level. To be plain, the way this company did business drove me nuts!

I really did make an effort to be a success in that company, but I didn't even know what game we were playing, let along the rules. I once confided in another employee, "I would love to play their game, if I only knew the rules."

His answer to me was, "The first rule is that there are no rules."

Seriously? In that moment, I understood that I needed to start my own business. I had no idea what it would be, just that it was a necessity. There was no way I could work like that for an entire career. I needed to be in charge of my own destiny. From my perspective, the management in my office was crazy and untrustworthy.

My intent is not to denigrate people who work in hierarchical corporate environments. Rather to illustrate that my soul is wired differently and our schematics were incompatible. For people with different gifts, their way works. Obviously, that's true, as a great many people find success and satisfaction in such situations.

Having come to the startling realization that I needed to be my own boss, but not understanding why, I judged myself as being in some way defective. Why were all these other people able to make the company's practices work for them when I could not? It would be many years before I was able to throw off that misplaced, negative judgment of myself and my value structure.

At this point, I will interject that if you're nodding your head with understanding you probably have the same or a similar gift as me. If not, rest assured that your divine gift has its own delicious idiosyncrasies.

Enter the Akashic Records

It was many years later when I received an Akashic Records reading from a talented reader that all the pieces fell into place. There was nothing wrong with me! The reason I felt as I did was due to the way my soul is wired! You see, it turns out some of the characteristics of my divine gift include being independent and strong willed, leadership, and a natural sense of entrepreneurship. *Ahhh...* now the light bulbs were coming on!

Those were just the earliest discoveries I made. There have been so many more since then that I now understand myself in a way I didn't even realize was possible. It was as if someone introduced me to my soul, and as the poet Robert Frost might say, that has made all the difference. My journey has been altered in the very best, most exciting ways.

Learning that I had a divine gift was a massively liberating and empowering insight for me, which is why I'm passionate about helping other people discover their divine gifts by reading their Akashic Records for them. Knowing your gift is like having all your birthday and Christmas presents rolled into one—and then some!

With understanding came acceptance and deep appreciation of myself. Because of this, I consider the day I learned the nature of my divine gift the real beginning of my journey to acquiring self-worth and helping others value themselves similarly.

The dramatic change the revelation of my gift made in my life was magical. It was something I had never expected or thought possible. Embodying it didn't happen overnight. But it did happen. Transformation takes time.

Since receiving a reading of my records, I've read the Akashic Records for a great number of other people. Each time I have the honor and privilege of introducing someone to his or her soul in this way, it's magical. The delight and wonder of meeting your soul nearly defies description.

When people learn their gifts, they always marvel at how a stranger could explain them to themselves in a way that made so much sense. Light bulbs go off, insights explode, and their perceptions of themselves are transformed. They get crystal clarity. Questions they didn't even know they had are answered. There's a rush of aha moments and insights. The experience is deeply profound.

Sometimes people even describe having physical sensations during a reading because their energy shifts as new understanding sinks in. Doors in their minds blow open so that new possibilities and ideas can flow in.

That's transformational.

Answers to Every Question

In my business as an Akashic reader, I call myself the Answer Diva. The answers to any question you could ask are contained in your Akashic Records. My job is to retrieve, translate, and relay those answers to you. The answers may not always be what you're expecting, but they *will* be exactly what you need. That's the genius of how the records were designed. The Akashic Records hold complete truth, light, and pure love for the magnificent creation that is you.

Rules of Access

You or someone you designate can enter your Akashic Records to research your soul. Whether you're searching for details on how past-life experiences are reverberating through the present, or you have questions about the underlying meaning of current situations, the archive is available with all the information you need.

We are not allowed to access the records of random people unless we have their permission, which is how experts like me are able to access *your* records.

There are even Akashic Records attached to physical addresses. If you own or otherwise have legal rights to a home or property, this location's records are available to you. If there's an address, there's an energetic history, and thus, Akashic Records. Reading for spaces where you live can be incredibly helpful if there are negative energetic issues that need to be resolved.

If you own a business, you'll be glad to know that businesses also have Akashic Records as soon as they begin generating revenue. You or a reader you have designated for this purpose are permitted to access these records. It can be incredibly helpful to look for energetic misalignments to help your business quickly get back on track. Do you need help choosing the best logo, or making marketing decisions? Consult the archive and get fast, definitive answers about whether your tactics are energetically aligned with you. Why would you ever guess when you can get a definitive answer?

When I read for a client, I am interfacing with a group of energetic beings known collectively as *Akashic guides*. Each Akashic archive has an entire team whose job is to serve their human in any way they can without interfering with free choice. These teams are overseen by Archangel Metatron, the grand master of the Akasha.

During readings, I receive information in several ways. Much of it is visual, like watching a movie, but all my senses are engaged. I may touch, smell, taste, or intuitively feel the message. Your guide team will use whatever method is most effective to convey a message. It's always true and immediately actionable.

Wisdom of the Akasha

I encourage you to seek the wisdom of the Akashic Records with an open mind. You may ask for whatever is most important for you to know at a given time, or you may ask specific questions. Akashic guides are exemplary teachers. When I read for my clients, they frame their message in a way that is most impactful for the intended recipient. They nearly always include one or more bits of information that serve as validation for the client.

For instance, in one reading I was kneeling on broken glass. It was extremely painful and yet I stayed there, even moving around upon it. The glass I saw was red, blue, and green, and looked like shards of broken wine bottles. When I described this vision, my client immediately understood the message. Her mother was an alcoholic and wine was her drink of choice. Kneeling on the glass represented the way that my client unconsciously punishes herself.

Occasionally, information about the universe, time, or other concepts is shared. Sometimes I don't fully understand parts of a message, as my consciousness hasn't yet caught up with the teaching. Nonetheless, I pass along the exact message I have received as clearly as I possibly can. I trust my understanding will eventually grow, as I download and learn more from the records all the time. What matters is that the person for whom a message was intended understands it.

I am a translator, downloading whatever wisdom the guides wish to share. Often messages are intended to be shared with whomever has ears to hear. The wisdom is being disseminated for the benefit of as wide an audience as I can bring it to. Messages of a sensitive nature, on the other hand, are private and must remain that way. Discretion is an important component of my work.

Sometimes stories from a person's past lives will spontaneously come through. When that happens, it's time for the individual to gain a deeper understanding of a related issue. The purpose of doing research in the Akashic Records is not to dig into past lives merely for curiosity's sake, it's about learning, growing, and expanding your consciousness. For that reason, details that are given us by the guides generally are concise and specific.

Of course we can't change what has happened in our past lives, we can only learn from it and use it to help us move forward in a more empowered fashion.

The most important thing to understand when you receive a message from the guides is that everything that comes from your Akashic Records is truth, shared with the intent of helping you on your journey to higher consciousness.

One of the many things I love about the Akashic guides is their total nonjudgment of our choices and beliefs. It doesn't matter what you believe or where you have come from. The absolute truth is that the Creator gave you an archive of your energetic history and makeup to empower and guide you on your journey. What you do with the knowledge is totally up to you.

This wisdom was shared by the guides of the Akasha to help one of my clients step up as an empowered soul. It equally applies to every one of us:

You did not come to rest upon your laurels. You came to experience vitality, vigor—to feel the life force surging through every cell of your body. To experience exhilaration, wondrous events, and experiences that would test and temper you like fine steel. You came with an ambitious agenda. It was a big assignment, but one you chose and eagerly anticipated. You knew it would not be easy, but you knew that with great struggle comes great achievement. And you embraced the challenge.

From your current perspective, the challenge of this life journey may seem insurmountable, however you can trust that you knew what you were doing and all is as it should be. Ride the bull for the full eight seconds. You CAN do it!

Come to the well of the Akasha, drink deeply and as often as you require to maintain your focus and momentum. We will always be here to guide, support, and cheer you on. Whatever you need . . . come to the well.

CHAPTER TWO

SOUL PURPOSE

Most of us have an innate urge to pursue our purpose. We have an idea that when we finally figure out a larger, higher purpose, we'll know what to do with our lives—particularly what career to pursue.

Being

I remember during high school that most of us were trying to figure out what we wanted to "be" when we grew up. Adults were always asking, "What do you want to be?" Meaning, "What job do you want to have?" There was a lot of angst around the concept of *being*.

Do you remember Dustin Hoffman in *The Graduate*? His character, Benjamin, a twenty-two-year-old recent college graduate, got a heavy dose of pressure from his parents and their friends to determine what he was going to be, and look how that turned out!

Spoiler alert: First, he had an affair with a woman his mother's age, and then he ran away with her daughter. But he never found a job.

With the Akashic Records, Benjamin could have eliminated all of that angst.

As it turns out, we had it all wrong back in the day. None of us must "be" anything. Our purpose is to use our divine gifts (given to us by our Creator), while having a human experience. In so doing, our souls are continually seeking higher consciousness. If we choose to follow that path, everything else will fall into place.

I'm not saying you don't have to be concerned with earning a living, because obviously you need to support yourself. But if you first seek to understand how your unique combination of gifts work and then apply that understanding to being whatever you choose to be, you'll find more success, satisfaction, and happiness in any career or purpose you choose to pursue.

Life is all about finding what feeds your soul. What delights your senses? Figure that out, and then go and do more of it. That's the simple recipe for life. Find what nourishes your soul and do more of that.

For me, the answer to the question of what to do for a living was first to empower myself, and then to help others become empowered. That feeds *my* soul. I can choose to help others in any way that pleases me. The way I have chosen is reading the Akashic Records. It's the fastest, most effective way I've found to live my purpose—to *be*. It was only after discovering my gifts that I understood and found this path.

So, you see, your soul purpose is not to *be* a certain kind of professional. It's to be the best you in a way that helps others and that will feed your soul. When you realize how you can help others, and nourish your soul, you'll never settle for anything less professionally ever again.

Divine Gift or Superpower?

Every soul is endowed with one or more divine gifts, which I like to call super powers. You won't know your gift or gifts until your records are read.

Why do I call a divine gift a super power? Because when you know what your divine gift is and master it, you'll become nearly unstoppable. Using your gift is when you will be fully empowered, your life will flow, and you will manifest with ease. Informing you of this fact compelled me to write this book. You *need* to know this so that you can start flexing your super hero muscles and begin living your purpose.

It's human nature to take our gifts for granted because they've always just been there. We are born with them. However, until you understand how to make your gift work *for* you, life will be more challenging than it needs to be. Your gift is part of who you are, just as mine is a part of who I am. Understand, all people have their own. And what comes natural to one person will be quite different than what comes natural to you and me. Most of us go around thinking our normal is everyone else's normal, but it's truly not. We're one-of-a-kind creations.

Planet Earth is presently undergoing an energetic transformation, which makes it more important than ever for you to consciously use your gift for the benefit of yourself and others. Every living being upon the Earth must transform as well or be left in the dust—perhaps literally. The choice is yours: transformation or dust?

Archangel Metatron, calls this global energy shift the *cosmic wave of transformation*. You can read more about it on my website, AkashaUnleashed.com.

Maintaining Energetic Balance

Once you're effectively using your divine gift for yourself and to serve others, you will be in energetic balance. Expressing your soul purpose brings you into energetic alignment, or balance. But be mindful, each gift has challenges that can easily throw you right out of balance again. Much like a gymnast negotiating a balance beam, if you veer too far left or right you risk falling off. *Ouch!*

Each divine gift comes with a set of characteristics that presents the opportunity for you to have, do, or *be* anything you want. It's *your* journey, so it's *your* choice what to do specifically with your life, just remember that balance is a crucial factor in creating success and happiness.

Your soul is wired for you to express your super power. Tapping into a divine gift is the path to creating a magnificent life. Isn't that what we all long for?

And it turns out it's much easier than we ever imagined when we tune in and use the tools the Creator gave us: the Akashic Records.

Using your divine gift in a conscious manner brings you into energetic alignment with your soul. From then on, instead of stumbling through life wearing blinders about who you truly are, you'll have clarity of vision and purpose, allowing you to make the most empowered choices possible and lead an extraordinary life.

Rather than guessing, I highly encourage you to consult your Akashic Records either yourself or through an intermediary like me.

To demonstrate the importance of knowing your divine gift, let me tell you about Teresa. When I shared with her that her gift was primarily about finding and creating order, she felt I must be incorrect. She didn't consider herself an organized or orderly person. As we probed deeper, however, it became crystal clear that this was in fact her gift. She had been spinning her wheels in frustration for quite some time because she was way out of energetic alignment. She was intuitively drawn to create more order in her life, so had been purchasing lots of schedulers, journals, planners, and similar items. The need was there, and she was trying to meet it. What she lacked was follow through. Without it she was seriously stuck.

With the clarity of knowing her purpose was to bring order, she quickly began acting to organize her life. In a humorous twist, she reported to me that in January that year she had chosen the word *order* as her focus word for the year. It seems her soul had been a step ahead of her, already preparing the way. Don't you love that?

Here is what Teresa said about her Akashic reading.

Thank you so much for the reading. My mind has been buzzing ever since we talked.

I'm thinking of some of the things I've done through the years to try to achieve order: like buying tons of organizing products, bins, boxes, shelves, sorters, journals, notebooks, and so on. Then I put them away and don't use them because I haven't found the perfect system for organizing. I have stacks of notebooks and journals that don't get written in because I want to make sure to match the right notebook with the right subject matter. Or I start writing in one notebook and then decide that topic should be in a different one. Knowing where this comes from really helps me see it in a new light. Not as a fatal flaw, but as my soul trying to find order and beauty, even if I am going overboard with it to the point of paralysis.

Odd that knowing this makes me feel like I can finally tweak my behavior; maybe because I feel that it only needs tweaking and I do not need to do a major overhaul of who I am.

CHAPTER THREE

ALL BECAUSE OF A HORSE

From an early age, I felt a burning desire to know my soul purpose. I knew there was something I was "supposed to" accomplish during my lifetime, but what?

Searching for My Soul Purpose

As I look back, it strikes me as funny that I don't remember ever discussing my desire to know my soul purpose with anyone. It was just always with me, nagging at the back of my psyche. Like so many others, I thought it had something to do with a job.

During that time, I noticed that sometimes I would "know" things. Intuitively. I had no idea how. The information was just there, and I knew

33

it to be true. I didn't think too much about it, because I thought everybody experienced that kind of knowing.

Throughout my life, I would occasionally see visual vignettes in my head while talking with someone. I never said anything about it to anyone, because I thought it happened to everyone.

It seems quite comical to admit this now. Oh, if I had only had a mentor to help me understand that what I had been experiencing was a divine gift, something to treasure and put to use, how different my life might have been!

But fear not. Everything was about to change... all because of a horse.

A Pennsylvania Country Girl Goes to Brooklyn

I saw her picture on the internet and was instantly smitten. There she was: my dream horse, my Black Beauty. Her name was Scenic Mist. It didn't matter that she lived seven hours away from me. It didn't matter that she was untrained. I. Had. To. Have. Her.

It was the early 2000s.

I was living in Brooklyn, New York, running a successful database consulting business. As a kid, I'd had a horse I adored and always planned to get one again. Years then passed, until one day I confronted the sobering realization that if I didn't get a horse soon I probably never would. Act now vs. regret it forever.

After falling for the internet picture of Scenic Mist (Misty), I flew out to meet her, purchased her, then started making the arrangements to bring her to Brooklyn. First, I went to a stable just blocks from my home and arranged to rent a stall. Then, I hired a professional shipper to transport her.

That's when the trouble started. You see, although the breeder had taken great pains to imprint Misty as a foal, they had forgotten to teach her one vitally important thing: how to calmly walk unto a horse trailer.

Horses are prey animals. To them a trailer is like going into a dark cave. And for all they know, the cave could be inhabited by a cougar. Going into a trailer or any dark, enclosed space, is not natural for horses. They must be trained to trust their handler, ignore their instincts, and enter.

This one massive oversight was to change the trajectory of my life, the horse's life, and my family's lives.

A Tragic Trip

There I was, in Brooklyn, anxiously awaiting the arrival of Misty, blissfully unaware of what had transpired. She arrived a day later than expected. When the trailer *finally* pulled in, the horse in the trailer was a different one than the girl I had met. She was shaking, jittery, her eyes were glazed over, and she had rope burns on her hind legs. Looking back on it now, I understand that she had the equine version of post-traumatic stress disorder. At the time I was just concerned with calming her down and getting her settled in her new stall.

As I spoke with the shipper, the story came tumbling out. When he had showed up at the farm to get her, she'd refused to get on the trailer. He and the breeder had coaxed, pushed, and shoved. But she fought against them as if her life depended on it, because in her mind it did. They finally managed to brute force her into that trailer, which is where the rope burns on her back legs had come from.

Once inside, she proceeded to do everything in her power to destroy the trailer. At this point, they finally decided to tranquilize her, but terrible damage had already been done—physically and mentally.

I can only imagine what was going through her mind at the time. She was being brutalized, shoved into a moving box, and taken to who knows where. It would be months before I learned the full extent of the damage that had been done.

At that point, Misty was only halter trained, so I went every day to groom her and walk her around the bridle trail in Prospect Park. An oasis of 526 acres of public land in the heart of Brooklyn, the park boasts three and a half miles of bridle trails. But there was no turnout (fenced-in space), for horses to romp and play, either at the stable or in the park, so this was the only exercise she got. Our walks became an extreme sport, as she bit, kicked, reared, and struck at me.

Since her fateful trip, Misty had become a nasty, bad-tempered girl. The staff had to keep the top door of her stall closed, as she would try to bite anyone who walked by. She also tried to kick anyone who entered her stall. This was not the same horse. She seemed intent on killing me and anyone else who got in her way.

The first clue that Misty had been enduring physical pain came from the farrier, the man at the stable who cared for the horses' hooves through trimming and shoeing them. This equine "pedicurist" noticed that Misty had a problem. I am so thankful for him as no one else had noticed that before, least of all me. I didn't know what I didn't know—and it was a lot!

Based on this new information, I brought the vet in. He first recommended acupuncture treatments. We tried needling the horse a few times, but it only seemed to make matters worse. Then,

I found a human chiropractor, Concetta Butera, D.C., who was also a horsewoman, and she agreed to look at Misty.

Now we were getting somewhere. Dr. Butera explained that when Misty was forced onto the trailer, it threw her pelvis out, along with some ribs and vertebrae.

The doctor began Misty's treatment by offering her some Reiki healing on her rump and got kicked for her trouble. It took bravery, creativity, and commitment to perform the first two chiropractic adjustments on the horse after that.

Another healer I brought in to help Misty was a massage therapist, who essentially told me I was crazy and should get rid of the horse or send her elsewhere for professional training. Although I disregarded this opinion, an important thing came out of our meeting, even though the pieces didn't come together until sometime later. The massage therapist observed that I was really tuned in to my horse because I knew what she felt about certain things.

Years later, after I had reconnected with my intuitive gift, this comment made more sense. At the time, I had just thought that I was paying attention to subtle clues. Didn't everyone? No, apparently not, as it turns out.

I was determined to get Misty well so we could have fun together. But she was the most difficult horse I'd ever met, and I needed help. Once her pain had been eased by chiropractic care, she was more approachable.

After some false starts with training, I discovered Parelli Natural Horsemanship and began their self-study course. Founded and taught by Pat and Linda Parelli, this is a philosophy of training horses using gentle, nonviolent means. With Parelli, the trainer looks at the world from the horse's point of view, allowing the horse to have an opinion, rather than forcing it to obey. Using the same nonverbal language that horses use with one another combined with persuasive psychology, results in extremely effective communication between human and horse. Horses appreciate being respected as sentient beings. Whey they feel understood, they are calmer, happier, and more willing to engage with their human partners.

Now, Misty and I were making progress! Among other things, the course taught how to use body language to communicate. Within two weeks of working things out on my own, Misty was a changed horse. Aside from the pain, it turned out that she was an alpha mare, a born herd leader, which meant that if the human that handled her didn't persuade her she was a competent leader, Misty would take over. She hadn't been trying to kill me, she'd been putting me in my place: below her in the herd hierarchy.

Imagine if you went to a foreign country where you didn't speak the language, and no one spoke yours. You might feel isolated, lonely, frightened, and a whole host of other emotions, and that doesn't yet factor in being in pain. Then one day someone comes along and speaks your language. How relieved, happy, and grateful would you be? That's essentially what happened with the new training. I was now speaking Misty's language. She breathed a huge sigh of relief and relaxed.

Once we could have a "conversation," we became partners. We spent a year walking the trail in the park nearly every day. I did a lot of ground training with her as we walked, which includes essential skills like leading with a halter, backing up, moving sideways, yielding the hindquarters or forequarters on command—and the infamous trailer loading. Essentially, I taught her to move where, when, and how I and her other handlers directed. Ground training builds a respectful relationship and allows horses to be safely handled. This is the best preparation for saddle training, since a relationship of cooperation has already been established.

It wasn't long before Misty would back up with just the wiggle of my finger. I sent her sideways along fences, eventually getting a canter, which was exciting for me. When it was time to saddle train, Misty already had a lot of skills, so it went smoothly.

During the ordeal with Misty, I had studied all kind of things, trying to find ways to help her. One of them was animal communication. I hired a communicator who remarked that Misty was very guarded and difficult to connect with. She did get some information, which was helpful, but I knew there was more, so I wanted to be able to talk to her myself. I adore my girl and wanted to do everything I could to make her happy.

Animal Communication: A Door Opens

At the time I took the animal communication course, I was not yet what some would call a woo-woo person. Quite the opposite. I had no familiarity with metaphysics. So, when we began by invoking the spirits of each direction on the compass, I was silently freaking out, wondering what I had gotten myself into.

Later, the teacher conducted a little ceremony with burning sage, a shamanic practice to cleanse the energy of the space known as *smudging*. I did not like that at all. Because I grew up with a parent who smoked, my body reacts to any form of smoke by trying not to breathe. While the other members of our circle deeply inhaled the smoke, I passed the burning sage bundle quickly to the person next to me.

Much to my surprise, I could easily complete the exercises during class and connect with animals, including some that were present only in spirit. It was surprisingly effortless. As the day-long training progressed, I connected more quickly each time.

Of course, not all the information I gleaned could be validated, but some of it could, and not just for me, but for most of my classmates. Today I understand that most people have some psychic ability; they just need a little help to activate it.

Our last exercise was to select an animal to connect with as a class. I had shared enough of Misty's story that everybody was eager to take her on and see what answers might be discovered.

What we learned is that she was still majorly pissed off at being abruptly taken from the only home she'd ever known and made to leave her family behind, and nobody had bothered to ask if it was okay with her. Imagine that?

It had never occurred to me that we should ask. I grew up on a farm where animals came and went all the time. We humans can be oblivious at times.

With her revelation, Misty's request was that I not send her away and promise to keep her for a long time. I didn't, and I have.

Following the Bread Crumbs:
The Hindsight Perspective

What does all this have to do with the Akashic Records?

I already told you that as a child I would just know things. It was my normal, and I had no idea it wasn't the same for everyone. At some point I must have subconsciously realized my sensitivity wasn't typical and suppressed it. The animal communication class reactivated my gift. As a result, I had a new purpose and started communicating with many animals to exercise my psychic muscles.

That was fun, but I found it hard to trust the information that came through. Eventually I decided that if I could talk to animal spirits, I surely could talk to human spirits, so I ventured into the practice of mediumship.

Mediumship was interesting. I connected with several deceased friends and family (people now in spirit) and got lots of questions answered. These conversations gave me a real understanding of what happens after death. It was fascinating, but still not ringing my bell.

One day I was listening to Esther Hicks channeling a spirit guide named Abraham, who was encouraging a lady in Hicks's audience to try channeling. They assured her she could do it—

saying that, in fact, everyone can. This remark resonated strongly with me, so I thought, *Okay, Abraham, I will.* And I did.

When I tried to channel, I quickly connected with a group of energetic beings and discovered I could receive messages. They said I could call them whatever I liked, so I dubbed them (as a unit) Charlotte, after my beloved grandmother. I channeled Charlotte for a while, but struggled with trusting what came through, just as I had with animal communication.

Next, I listened to several virtual summits where the Akashic Records were a topic. That piqued my interest. One of the presenters was Linda Howe, founder and director of the Center for Akashic Studies. I ordered and devoured her book *How to Read the Akashic Records,* and using her Pathway Prayer, dived into reading the Akashic Records myself.

Whoa, this was a very different experience from talking to animals or the Charlotte consciousness! The messages came through in allegorical form. They were entertaining narratives that connected to a central story. It seemed phenomenal to me how details that at first seemed unrelated ultimately connected perfectly.

My Akashic Experience

When I enter the Akashic Records, very often I see a door. Usually the door opens easily, but sometimes I must pull forcefully on it. When there is this necessity, it's because the person I'm reading for is afraid or reluctant to find out what their guides have to say. This is just one of many fascinating details I've discovered during my Akashic explorations.

Once beyond the door, the visuals can be anything. Often, the scene is pastoral; there may be a pond or brook and trees. Sometimes it's mountainous. Occasionally, I find myself in outer space. One time I stepped into the ocean. The locations truly run the gamut.

After I absorb the setting, I move forward in whichever direction feels right. In fairly short order, I encounter one or more guides who may come in human, animal, or mythical creature form. In my own records, a green dragon named Elissa has made numerous appearances.

When I use the term *spirit guides,* or just *guides,* this is my generic reference for the beings I encounter in the Akashic Records. They may be masters, teachers, angels, or spirit guides. There's no need for distinction, as they all function as messengers, although I have observed that there is a hierarchy. For instance, Ezekiel is my help desk guide. His specialty is data retrieval. Story-telling comes from higher-ranked guides, except when it's something extra important. Then arch-angel Metatron may step in.

Once a guide or guides appear, the story begins. In one memorable reading, I traveled through space passing by a cluster of pink stars, waved at the Little Prince on his planet, and eventually ended up standing before the obelisk from the film *2001: A Space Odyssey*. Peculiar as that all sounds, it was deeply meaningful for my client. The imagery of a reading doesn't have to make sense to me, I just need to carefully translate every detail so that my client can understand the message.

One thing has remained constant, I still find it astonishing what incredible storytellers the guides of the Akasha are.

Although the Pathway Prayer enabled me to easily access the records when I started my readings, after a time I felt the need for something more and began seeking a new form of connection. I had heard about an ancient Mayan prayer that some people were using to access the records, but it wasn't freely shared. It took some sleuthing before I finally found it. This prayer felt more comfortable, and in using it, I noticed an immediate change in the messages. They were deeper, more profound. I experimented, alternating prayers for a short while, then I asked my guides to explain why there was a difference in my experience.

Apparently, there is no right or wrong way to connect to the records. From the guides, I learned that there are a multitude of access portals. The experience and message will reflect the portal. Since then, I have been inspired to write my own prayer, which I now teach to those who want to access their own records.

Akasha Unleashed Is Born

Once I had a taste of the Akashic Records, I was on fire to do more readings, so I contacted some friends, offered to read for them, and asked them to send me other people to read for. I needed practice. That was a phenomenal experience! The messages the guides were giving me kept getting longer and more detailed. People really resonated with the messages I was delivering for them.

One friend I reached out to was Ariel, whom I'd met at the Brooklyn stable. Her horse, Prospero, had been kept in the stall across from Misty. The horses were mad about each other. We'd both moved far from Brooklyn by then, but we'd kept in touch. Ariel graciously introduced me to some people who were happy to let me practice on them.

Akashic messages generally contain layers of meaning. When I read, each message comes to me with some sort of information that can be used for validation of its authenticity. This enables my clients to relax and trust that they are hearing the truth. Reading the Akashic Records for Ariel's friend Cili was a pivotal moment for me. Cili is spiritually conscious and wise. During her reading she taught me to interpret the symbolism of the allegorical messages, and that was transformational.

Very quickly, I understood that reading the Akashic Records was what I had been searching for all my life. This was my soul purpose! I had finally come home. Soon after that, I founded my company, Akasha Unleashed.

In one of my meditations, a spirit guide came to me in the form of Martin Luther King, Jr. Here is a small portion of the message he imparted.

There is a thread that runs through all of life connecting disparate people and events. When a stitch gathers up a person, place, or time in that manner, it creates a "throughness" connecting everyone and everything along that timeline. How they are affected is not always obvious and the how may not even be important for you to understand. The important lesson here is the interconnectedness of people, places, and events. As you follow your bread crumbs, you will become more acutely aware of this truth, and you will see even more clearly that which you need to see. Think of it as giving you Sherlock Holmes-style sensitivity. This process is about honing your senses so that you do not miss the subtle clues. It's fine tuning your entire being so that you are in alignment with your soul purpose.

CHAPTER FOUR

GET OUT OF YOUR HEAD AND INTO YOUR SOLAR PLEXUS

Now that you have a better understanding of what this life journey is all about, and how the Akashic Records can help you make choices in life, it's time to focus on the elephant in the room: the EGO. As you'll learn in this chapter, our egos mean well, but they are very misguided. It's time to shed some light on the old ego and its sneaky ways, so we can make friends and have great lives together.

Self-appreciation

You are a magnificent soul: brilliant, perfect, and even resplendent. That's the truth of who you are. This is a common theme I hear from the spirit guides of the records, because so many of us need

51

to hear it. And even more importantly, we need to *believe it.*

Acknowledging that you are wonderful is not about stroking your ego. It's about helping you come to terms with how amazing you are. It's time to stop selling yourself short and underestimating your potential.

Your Akashic guides want you to know:

Greatness is within you. That is said not to inflate your ego, but rather to inspire humbleness at the task you have before you. You should understand that you, yourself, chose the path you are on before you inhabited your body. You are simply fulfilling the purpose that you intended for yourself. You are much blessed and loved, and we want you to know that observing how you are walking your path brings us great joy. Go forth and spread your light throughout the world with peace and love. Amen.

Now, keeping in mind how amazing your Akashic guides say you are, it's important to acknowledge that elephant in the room. If we are not consciously aware of the shenanigans that dear old ego can get up to, it may wreak havoc in our lives. Balance in all things is the ideal to strive for.

To that end, some of us have spent decades trying to make friends with our ego. We coddled it and cooed to it "you're ok." That emboldened ego to the point where it took full advantage and began running us around by the nose.

Having entered a relatively enlightened age, we now understand that a healthy ego is important, but it can be a hindrance if it's allowed to totally run the show. A healthy ego is supposed to establish boundaries and preserve our lives. It only wants to keep us safe and comfortable our entire lives, like being in a warm, cozy, cocoon from which we never emerge. The trouble is that it acts like an anchor; it keeps us from elevating our consciousness by discouraging us from taking new actions.

If you wish to raise your vibrational frequency enough to reach higher consciousness, you *must* emerge from your protective cocoon and become the beautiful butterfly you were destined to be. It is your choice, of course. You have the option to stay safe and experience little expansion during your lifetime. If so, you will begin your next incarnation at almost the same place you started this one. But doesn't that seem like a waste of a good life? It does to me.

To undergo transformation, or not, is always your choice.

If you're reading this book, I'm presuming you're more than a little bit interested in higher consciousness. Your soul has awakened, you're hungry for more information and wish to increase your vibrational frequency. What then are you to do about our friend, the ego, who keeps putting on the brakes?

We want to be kind. The ego is well intentioned. It's a biological part of us, so we can't discard it. How about making friends and negotiating a truce?

Your ego (a function of the brain), higher self, and soul need to find a way to work in harmony. Each aspect of who you are has a very different idea about your life journey. Ego carries about your third-dimensional earthly life: finances, status, safety, and appearances. The higher self—which is your fourth-dimensional aspect—cares about your expanding awareness. And your soul—which is your fifth-dimensional aspect—cares about reaching ever higher consciousness. Therefore, if you're like most people, there's often a tug of war going on between your ego and soul, with your higher self playing the role of rope. That's not productive.

Three Parts of a Whole

Understanding about the three distinct parts of self was a lot to wrap my head around, so I went to the Akashic Records seeking clarity. On this day, my guide Elissa, a green dragon, brought the message.

When the three parts of self are in harmony, life flows effortlessly. But when they are out of balance, trouble begins. Then life may feel like riding stormy seas.

The three parts of self (ego, higher self, and soul) are intrinsically linked. When they are in balance, all things are possible. Otherwise you are trying to brute force your will upon the world. That will only result in doors closing before you. When you are in harmony, all lights are green, all doors are open."

I followed up by asking Elissa: "How do I keep them in balance?" And she replied:

Ah that's the challenge. Ego may try to steamroll the other two parts, but doing so creates waves in your pond. When you feel the waves, realize that you are out of harmony, then take a moment to regroup and rebalance.

I continued my inquiry, by asking: "What techniques or actions must I take to achieve harmonic balance?"

Elissa replied:

You must feel your way into it. Take a step, check for balance. If you're balanced keep going and checking. If you're out of balance, course correct immediately. Do not wait for a typhoon to form, for then you may find yourself struggling to stay afloat in a tsunami of your own making.

Ask your ego and soul to work with you. Listen to what they say. You are the driver and they are the passengers, but that does not mean that you can, or should, make all the decisions.

Answers from the Akasha

At the time I engaged in this dialogue, the message felt good and seemed clear, but in the ensuing days, confusion crept back in. I still wasn't entirely sure how to tackle the problem of balancing the three parts of self. My motto is: If it's not clear, go back and ask for more guidance.

So that's just what I did. This time I asked for clarity about balance. What exactly did she mean about balancing the three aspects of self and how was I to accomplish this balance?

The conversation took place while I walked along a path near a wooded area, Elissa was again the Akashic messenger, and she was in a playful mood. She came to me in the form of Galadriel, the Elven character played by actress Cate Blanchett in the film trilogy based on J.R.R. Tolkien's book *The Lord of The Rings*. She said:

It is a conundrum to be sure. Seeking something for which you have no insight or experience. Something totally new. How do you begin? What do you do?

I saw her put a finger to her lips. She then went on:

Shhh. Listen. The answer is before you, it always was, simply waiting for you to ask the question.

She looked at me expectantly, so I voiced my question: "How can humans bring the three aspects of ourselves into balance and harmony?"

Her answer was:

It is not something accomplished without effort. For some, it takes a lifetime. For others, it happens naturally because they allow it to be. For those like you, who are stubborn, strong willed, and often fight against their own best interests, it requires trust and letting go.

Remember. Allow. Do not force. Ask. Do not demand. Ask and expect it to be. It will come to pass, but not in your timing, as it is a cooperative effort. All three parts must want to work together for the greater good and their opinion of the greater good may be different than yours.

Then I asked, "Okay, so how do I engage with them to open negotiations?"

Elissa said:

Sit down and have a personal pow wow. Invite them to your party, entertain them. Show them you can be trusted to work with, not against them. Your parts all must understand that working cooperatively will not diminish any of you. Instead it will make you stronger and more effective.

Imagine the energy of a laser beam when it is concentrated and focused.

Working in harmony is like the Ghostbusters crossing their streams to amplify the power of their lasers. But understand that in that movie it was also their collective desire, intention, and focus that defeated their enemies. If any one of the group had been at cross purposes, they would have failed.

Let your soul dialogue with your ego and higher self. Find out what each aspect wants. Reach an understanding of the mission that will benefit all three.

I asked for additional insights. "Can you explain to me what the three aspects are? I wasn't entirely clear about that."

Elissa responded:

The three aspects are the ego/body, the higher self, and the soul. You must persuade the ego to stop stepping on the brakes, and you must persuade the higher self that your quest is of value to her goals.

You must not be at war with yourself. It is counterproductive and leads to great frustration.

I said, "I must say I feel ill equipped to negotiate with any of them."

She said:

I didn't say it would be easy. Nevertheless, it is the answer to that which you seek.

"Should I do that right now, or is there some preparation I need to do first?" I asked.

She replied:

Now is the perfect time.

As I thanked Elissa for her counsel, she leaned over, kissed me on the right cheek, and then vanished.

Hold a Meeting with Your Three Aspects of Self

Meeting with the three aspects of self is something we all have the power to do, and I highly recommend it. You may wish to try it yourself following a similar path to the one I took and will now share with you. During such pow wows, allow soul to lead and negotiate. Soul has a grander view of your purpose than the other two aspects.

Here is how my soul conducted a meeting based on Elissa's recommendation.

Seated in a comfortable position, I closed my eyes and allowed my consciousness to move up through my crown chakra into a space above my body. There, speaking from my soul aspect, I invited my higher self and ego to join me. When I opened my eyes in the vision, there were three of me present.

My higher self was alive with energy, which emanated from her and spiraled around her.

My ego was all buttoned up, energetically speaking. She was wearing a long, dark coat that was buttoned all the way to the throat, along with a bowler hat, perhaps to keep energy from escaping. Tall galoshes completed the outfit so that nearly the entire body of my ego was covered and protected. Encased, is what it felt like. I wondered if I could I persuade my ego to unwind a bit and maybe open a button or two. Take off the hat?

This is what was said.

Soul: "Thank you both for coming. I have just learned that for any of us to be successful in our endeavors, we must work together. I'm sorry I didn't understand this before, but I'm here now and pledge to do everything in my power to work with you toward a common goal that serves us all. What is it that you want?"

Ego: "I want to be safe, warm, and comfortable. I dislike being challenged or told what to do. Everything I have done has been for our mutual good. I'm a hard worker and don't like to be criticized."

Soul: "Thank you, Ego. I appreciate your efforts to keep us safe. We've gotten this far, so you've obviously done a good job. Do you think it's possible that you could loosen your grip just a little and allow the other two of us to contribute? Sometimes we are boxed in by your best of intentions. What if you relaxed and trusted us to work with you? Do you think that is possible?"

My ego didn't look happy.

Soul: "Ego, don't you see that you have done an excellent job of alerting us to dangers? You have kept us safe. But sometimes you've denied us opportunity for growth because you are so risk averse."

Ego: "It's for your own good."

Soul: "I appreciate your perspective, but could you allow that there are three of us here and it is unfair to ignore our input when making decisions?"

Ego (snarling): "Well, you try to push me around all the time."

Soul: "I'm sorry. I thought that was how it was supposed to be. I have only just learned that we are a cooperative and must find a way to function as one. Could you meet me part way?"

Ego: "Well if you're not going to stomp on me and ignore me, I might just be willing to consider easing up on the reins."

Soul: "Thank you, Ego. That is a wonderful start. And what about you, Higher Self? Would you be willing to contribute your perspective and work with us for our common good?"

Higher Self: "Well, what do you think I've been doing? There is so much I could share with you, if you'd only listen. But the two of you are always bickering and rarely give me a second thought. There have been times when you began a dialogue and I was so hopeful, and then you quickly reverted to ignoring me. It's heartbreaking."

Soul: "I'm sorry, Higher Self. I promise to ask for your input and allow you to participate in the decision making.

We had some further discussion about specific plans and goals with my ego and higher self each having their own say. Then I sat back and waited for their responses to my request to work as a unit.

My higher self looked excited and eager to try. My ego looked skeptical, but there was a gleam in her eye and I could see that the top two buttons of her coat were now open, and her hat was off. It felt like the moment when a man in a business suit loosens his tie. It's still there, but no longer restrictive.

These two parts of me seemed to be on board with my soul, even if there was still some lingering doubt. We put our palms together in a "Yay team" moment, and then parted ways to get started implementing our plan.

Readings such as these are highly visual experiences. On this occasion, I was left wondering if the agreement that had been made was enough. Was there something else I needed to do? Would this finally bring the three of us into harmony and balance? It still felt to me like there was some misalignment. In my mind's eye, I perceived this as a table with uneven legs.

Before I could end the meditation, my ego rushed back in and put a matchbook under one of the table's legs to even it out. I thought, *Yay, Ego. Now, that's teamwork!* My soul thanked her and with a big, happy smile she was off again.

It seemed as if our meeting was a great success and the collaboration was ripe with possibility. I invited Elissa back for confirmation. She appeared beaming and with a twinkle in her eyes. No words were necessary. I could see that she was pleased and giving her stamp of approval upon my efforts.

This message and process of dialoguing with all three aspects of self was incredibly helpful to me in learning to distinguish their voices. It gave me clarity about my ego's machinations. Since then I've remained alert to ensure that my ego isn't reverting to its old ways. That doesn't mean it never happens, but when it does, I feel the imbalance, and pause to sort things out. Gradually my ego has become more compliant and willing to go along with my soul and higher self, as she has observed that it ultimately works out well for her. When I check in on her, she appears to be feeling mighty fine about herself.

Using the Solar Plexus as a Tool

Now that you understand the importance of getting out of your head, let's talk about how you can connect with your solar plexus to discern your soul's truth.

You've surely heard people talk about "following" their gut or "getting a gut feeling." Whether they're consciously aware of it or not, they're really tapping into the internal compass, which is the solar plexus. This is something you should learn how to do too, for your solar plexus is where your truth lies.

Just what is the *internal compass?*

In your solar plexus, you possess an energetic compass, specially keyed into your soul's blueprint. This personal compass was meant to be used as a tool guiding you through life. Knowledge of this compass has largely been lost through the ages as humanity has become more enamored with abstract reasoning than its instincts. Instead of using this compass to feel our ways through life, we've substituted brain power.

When you think your way through life, it puts your ego in control. The problem with this is that your ego is concerned with keeping you safe, not with living a full, vibrant life. Sure, you can choose to settle if you like, and allow your ego to run the show. However, consider for a moment what would happen if you tuned into your compass and began feeling your way through life, as you were designed to do. Would your brain see the logic in doing that?

Think of checking in with your solar plexus as hitting the default switch and returning to original settings, before your soul and higher self got sidetracked by ego. When you begin feeling your way instinctually through your choices, life is going to get a whole lot more interesting for you, not to mention opening the door to the beautiful manifestations that are your soul's agenda for you.

In the beginning, feeling your way through life may be challenging. You may have misgivings and apprehensions. After all, you likely haven't been exercising this muscle in... forever. But I promise, if you stay the course and keep practicing, one day this mode of functioning will seem as natural as breathing. This is how you were designed to function!

Remember, you're reverting to your default settings.

Exercising Your Instinctual Muscles

When there is a decision to be made, focus on your solar plexus. How does it feel? In the beginning, you may notice very little, perhaps nothing at all.

Don't worry. It takes time to "tone a muscle." Of course, the solar plexus is a collection of nerves and not a muscle, but training yourself to check in with it for guidance is a lot like going to the gym. Your intuition will grow stronger the more you use it.

You may already be checking in with your solar plexus on an unconscious level, which is great. Now I'm going to encourage you to up the ante and do it deliberately, and consciously.

Ignore the whisperings of your ego, which may be telling you to mistrust your instincts, and keep your attention firmly focused upon your solar plexus.

If you feel an uncomfortable flutter or clenching sensation when you ask it a question, that's probably a no.

If you feel neutral, or a bit of excitement, that's probably a yes.

I recommend keeping a journal to track your experiences with guidance. That will help you recognize the difference between yesses and nos and really help you to "firm up" the "muscle" of your intuition.

Sometimes you'll be right, sometimes you'll be wrong. Part of this process is to build confidence in yourself. Don't get discouraged when you're wrong. In the beginning, it's very common to get more answers wrong than right. Keep checking in with your solar plexus and keep practicing. One day, you'll find it's quite easy to get your answers and more of those answers will be correct ones.

If you're wrong, simply stop what you're doing and make a correction.

The intuition is a crackerjack tool designed to help you navigate the complexities of life and avoid pitfalls. How unfortunate that its existence, and knowledge of how to get guidance from it, has been obscured through the ages. But now you know.

So you can use it.

If you get frustrated while attempting to access your compass, try meditation. It will help you tune in more fully, and you may find answers come easier.

Failing that, ask for help from someone who can read the Akashic Records. That's why there are professionals like myself. We can help people get answers when they're out of their reach. Often that help can serve to open a client's perception so that they begin having more success on their own. We all need a little help now and then.

Sometimes a client will come to me with a general, rather than specific, question. They are open to hearing whatever their guides have to share. Below is one such case. Perhaps it's the answer *you've* been seeking. When asked, "What should my main focus be for the new year?" the Akashic guides responded:

What would you like it to be? In other words, what would bring you the most joy? We encourage you to get very well acquainted with your internal guidance system. That's your solar plexus area. Focus in on what you feel there. Allow yourself to be guided more by feeling than by logic. Logic does not care a whit about your soul's purpose. It is like a robot. Very efficient for sure, but antiseptic and cold. You are not a robot; therefore, you would be better served by feeling your way toward the answer you seek.

If you find there are too many options to choose from, then pick just the one that feels best. If you cannot distinguish the best option, then, for goodness sake, flip a coin and give something a try. If after a time the option you're pursuing doesn't feel right, discard it and try another. Keep doing this until you find the solution that fits like a glove and feels like the most glorious day at Disneyland. Life is about adventure, excitement, exhilaration! Get some of that and you'll be cooking with gas. Oh yeah!

Are you getting the picture now? You get to decide everything in your life. No one else. You are the creator of your own destiny. Pick what brings you joy and do that, and do that, and do that, until you have finished with it, and then pick another thing to do that brings you joy. Your life experience is always about choice and how it makes you feel.

Remember to attune yourself to your guidance system. It will serve you well. For those times when you miss the boat, we'll be there to send a message to help you catch the next one.

CHAPTER FIVE

FREE CHOICE

As humans, we have absolute free choice. It's sacrosanct. Your team of Akashic guides will never interfere with your freedom of choice. That would be like violating the Prime Directive if you were a Federation officer on *Star Trek*.

Free Choice Is Universal Law

Wherever you are in your life is the result of the choices you have made. If you don't like where you are, make new choices. It's that simple. Archangel Metatron, overseer of the Akashic Records, has repeatedly shared this message when I'm doing readings, that's how important it is.

Understand that the choices you make today will create your tomorrow. If you want tomorrow to look different, then it would be wise to make different choices today.

This would be a good time to do some soul searching. Reflect on these questions.

- What's good in your life?
- How did you get there?
- What's *not* working?
- What choices led you there?

Also look for patterns where you've repeatedly gotten off track and life is decidedly going in the wrong direction. This information is important to your future well-being, so it's worth putting effort into this investigation.

If you're unable to identify patterns or can't see any way to make changes, try spending time in meditation. You can open yourself up to guidance in this way. Allow insights and clarity to flow. If this process doesn't work for you, then it may be time to consult an expert.

Please always remember that asking for help when you need it is like giving a gift to yourself. Get your answers and move on. Staying stuck and out of energetic alignment with your soul because you are unwilling to ask for help or take other measures to get unstuck is a recipe for a lackluster, disappointing life.

I've often described being out of alignment as driving down the highway with a flat tire. That makes for a bumpy ride and it will damage your car. Who would make that choice? No, you'd stop and get that flat fixed so you could get back to cruising smoothly along. Getting guidance really can be as simple as that.

We humans, for some mysterious reason, often like to make things more complicated than need be.

What If I Can't Choose?

Sometimes you may find yourself having too many appealing choices to choose between. You may be able to trim down your options to two or three, but can't bring yourself to rule any of them out as they all seem so delicious. When this happens, it's like spinning a car's wheels in the mud. You sink deeper and deeper while forward progress is halted.

On the one hand, it's wonderful to have many choices, but they do you no good if ultimately you can't make a decision. That's the absolute worst thing you can do. It shuts your manifestations right down and life gets a whole lot more "interesting" (and not in a good way) if you allow yourself to spin.

Remember the flat tire analogy?

When you find yourself in a state of indecision, give it your full attention. Stop, assess each choice. Tap into your solar plexus and feel your way through each option. Which feels best? Pick that one and get moving. You can always course correct later if you change your mind.

Sometimes you'll be unable to find "the right option." When this happens, the best thing you can do for yourself is to flip a coin or randomly choose, and then get moving. Quickly! After you've traveled the new path for a short while, reassess. Does it feel good? Yes? Keep going.

If it doesn't feel good, stop and *quickly* make another choice. You want to get back on a positive, empowering, and soul-aligned track as soon as possible.

The passage that follows came from a nameless Akashic guide and is part of a larger message. My client was really struggling to maintain her equilibrium as she navigated major life changes. It helped her tremendously to have an acknowledgment of her struggle and it gave her confidence to move forward.

The trajectory of your life path has taken a sharp right turn. You have entered unfamiliar territory and the footing may have a feeling of being uncomfortably uneven. We encourage you to keep moving forward, trusting that it will get smoother in short order. You will get your "sea legs," soon

enough. This is all a normal part of evolu-
tion and nothing to be alarmed about.

Anytime one ventures into new territory
there is a feeling of discomfort/ uneasiness.
That is how you will know that you are
evolving. If you were comfortable you
would be in a rut and that is no place for an
enlightened being.

Energetic Alignment

I've mentioned *energetic alignment* a few times now. In case you're not familiar with this concept, permit me to elaborate.

We're all composed of energy at the quantum level; science has proven this. Our energy has a vibrational frequency. Think of it like tuning into a radio station. Your frequency is a direct result of spiritual "work" you've done in both your past and present lives. The more work, the higher the frequency.

Being *in alignment* means that your soul and your third-dimensional self (which is connected to your ego) are broadcasting on the same frequency. That's living your soul purpose. In alignment, there's harmony and life flows smoothly.

Many people have yet to experience this incredible feeling. To them, life is just hard. They would say: "That's how it is. Best to accept it and live with it."

That's okay if they want to be complacent. Each of us is on an individual journey. Wherever we are on our journeys is perfect. One day, it will be "more perfect" when we've achieved even more alignment.

At first, alignment may only last for brief moments, but over time it will be sustained longer and longer until finally we spend more time in alignment than out of alignment. Alignment is the ultimate goal of our soul journeys.

Your soul's journey is about expansion and reaching higher consciousness. This means that any time you consciously decide to take a new, inspired action, your soul shifts to a new, higher frequency, taking it out of alignment with your egoic third-dimensional self.

As your soul frequency gets higher, it moves further out of alignment from your ego. The friction caused when this happens creates energetic "sparks" that wreak havoc in your world. This is the realm of dissonance. It can feel like walking on sticky paper. Each step takes greater effort. You've stopped flowing, you're struggling, you're bumping along on a flat tire. Your soul and ego are engaged in a vigorous tug of war. At the extreme, things could go *very* wrong. Dissonance is wicked and messes with your head.

Dissonance

It's not bad enough you have to contend with flat-tire syndrome, but on the other end of the spectrum, *dissonance* lies in wait. You're cruising along feeling wonderful, life is sweet. Then inspiration caresses your brow and you decide: Yes, indeedy, it's time to make my next quantum leap forward. You're feeling ready to step out of your comfort zone.

Taking inspired action causes your soul to shift to a higher frequency, meaning it's now out of alignment with your ego again. But this kind of misalignment is different from the flat-tire kind. This kind of misalignent creates friction, causing energy spikes that may influence things around you. Let's say energy bounces off you and runs smack dab into something like a kitchen appliance, a computer, or a car. If it does, it may cause a physical injury. Or suddenly you've got unexpected repairs to contend with. This may dampen your enthusiasm, and often it creates a financial hardship.

Little wonder that you begin questioning whether that inspired idea really *was* inspired. You think, *Maybe I misread the signs?* Your soul pleads, "Come on, we've got important things to accomplish." But your ego whispers her siren song: "It's a divine message that you're going the wrong way."

Dissonance accounts for a great many failures.

I am reminded of what happened many years ago when I tried water skiing. I was partway up and the water was blasting me in the face. I tried to hang in there and have this fun, new experience, but finally gave up because I panicked. Everyone said that if I'd only held on a bit longer I would have gotten up. But my survival instincts kicked in and said: "You must let go or you'll drown." That thought was very persuasive. I've learned a lot since then about hanging tough.

If I did not forewarn you about the voice of dissonance, then you might surrender too, slipping back into the safe, comfy space your ego wants to keep you in, abandoning your grand plans in the process when dissonance arrives.

It's vitally important to understand what dissonance looks and feels like so that you will recognize it when it happens and not be fooled—because it *will* happen.

Overcoming Dissonance

Okay, so now that you know how to recognize dissonance, what do you *do* about it?

Here's the good news. When you recognize the hot, stinky breath of dissonance on the back of your neck, you can celebrate. Really?!

Yes. Celebrate because it means you're on the right track. Then move faster to get through it as quickly as possible. If you do that, you'll come out the other side of your fear, arriving at a place where you can bask in the rewards of your accomplishments. In essence, you'll be up on your water skis and skimming across the crisp, cool water of your life with ease.

Take note and remember, because the next time you're ready for a big leap forward dissonance will be waiting to "spew water" in your face.

But guess what, this time you'll be prepared to kick dissonance's butt to the curb faster than ever before. You've got more important things to do than dance (or ski) with dissonance.

When we're in a state of dissonance, we don't usually think about consulting with the ego to bring her back into harmony with the soul and higher self. In my experience, it feels like survival mode and every woman for herself.

That said, it couldn't hurt to try. After you celebrate, you could also employ the meeting process outlined starting on page 60, if your ego will cooperate.

Dissonance Wreaks Havoc with Technology

Just in case you're still fuzzy about the potential ramifications of dissonance, here's a story of one of my more recent encounters with its friction.

I was planning to host some webinars in which I would offer group channeled readings to my community of past clients and online subscribers. But the idea stayed in the planning stages for a *very* long time because my ego found this to be a big, scary step. What if I got in front of the group and no messages came? What if no one wanted live readings? *What if... ? What if... ?*

Finally I pushed through the blocks and wrote a letter asking all those who were interested to email me an RSVP. Yay, I was finally taking new, inspired action to uplevel my life. What could go wrong? Enter dissonance!

In a disgusting display of incredibly bad timing, a glitch occurred at my internet hosting service. Anyone who responded to my email received a reply saying that no such email address as mine existed. I only found out that there was a technological snafu after several wonderful people contacted me on Facebook to let me know.

When I learned what had happened, I jumped into action and got tech support on the case. They found an errant switch that got flipped, or something like that. In any event, my emails began coming through again. Then, I quickly wrote another message apologizing and asking people to email me again. And my plans were set back into motion.

In the grand scheme of things, this was only a minor setback. Dissonance can and has done far worse in many people's lives. Like the time it caused my barn to collapse. You can read about that on my website (see Resources).

Now, that we've examined dissonance from all sides, it's time to move on. Just remember, you've been warned. Stay vigilant!

Where You Are in This Moment Is Perfect

It's important to understand that there is no judgment of you or your behavior from your Akashic team. Zero. Their entire purpose is to support you. When you connect with your guides, either on your own or through an intermediary, they will tell you that wherever you are right now is perfect because it's a result of choices that you've made. Some of those choices were good, some were not so good, but they were *your* choices.

You can change things up by making different choices anytime you like.

If you need help, call out to your guides. Your Akashic team is on standby, 24/7, to help you in any way they can. They're such enthusiastic supporters of you that at times they're literally whooping, shouting, and cheering you on. They put a lot of energy into getting your attention and helping you.

Understand that as soon as you call out they respond. They will persistently drop bread-crumbs in your path to get your attention (for example, showing you repeating numbers and other signs). If you think you've gotten a message, you probably did. Pay attention and act upon it. The more you do that, the more messages will come and the easier it will become to recognize them. More about this topic in a later chapter.

Now that you understand your guides see you as perfect already, please don't let that be an excuse to stop or discourage you from reaching for more and better. I hope you've gotten the message here that your life is about moving on out, *always* reaching for more and better.

What If I Don't See Any New Choices?

I get it. Sometimes we may feel so overwhelmed that we can't see the forest for the trees. We turn around and around and. . . nothing. We get nothing! The harder we try, the more nothing we get. At a time like this, your stress level rises, and you work yourself into a frenzy.

If this is happening to you, stop. Take a deep breath. Center and ground yourself. Take another deep breath. Allow yourself to relax. Call out to your guides and ask them for a sign. Then trust it will show up.

Signs can be visual, auditory, or just sensations. That's why they're so easy to miss. When you notice something and wonder if it's a sign, pause and focus on it. Feel it through your solar plexus. If you think it's a sign, go with it. And don't worry about it; if you're wrong, you'll find out soon enough.

Being centered and/or grounded means being present in your body. This will give you strong enough control that you won't be swept away by the personal energy of other people and of places. Just as electricity needs to be grounded to effectively conduct a current, so too does our energy need to be grounded so we may function effectively.

To center and ground yourself, you may visualize a pillar of white light coming down from above, entering the top of your head, traveling downward through your body, coming out your feet and penetrating deeply into the Earth. That's grounded.

If you meditate, you can do that to receive messages about new options. Get quiet. Listen. I promise, your guides are constantly sending you messages because they know from experience a great many are missed. They will *never* give up on you.

Very often when you're wondering whether it's a sign, it is. Try it. See where it takes you. Ride that wave for as long as it serves you. When it no longer does, make a new choice, ask for a new sign. Whatever feels appropriate at the moment. This is about exercising your intuitive muscle so that you can move forward while making choices with confidence.

In time, recognizing messages will happen with ease. Of course there will still be challenges, but you'll handle them and move on getting better and better, happier and happier. Raising your vibrational frequency. Manifesting with ease. *Ahhhhh,* that's what I'm talking about!

On one of my Akashic adventures I encountered Glinda, the Good Witch (of Oz fame). Glinda escorted me into the woods to meet a woman called Grandmother. She was a wise woman who offered a lesson and a message of encouragement.

It is enlightenment you seek and that is very good. You must always seek to expand your awareness of yourself and the world

*around you. Physical life is intended to pro-
vide a continuous stream of consciousness
raising, as it were. New experiences, sensations, ideas, thoughts, and energetic
transmissions. It is a race to soak up as
much new awareness and expansion as
possible before you recycle yourself back
from whence you came. You should not
waste opportunities that are presented because you are only delaying your own
expansion, and why would anyone in his or
her right mind do that? Why would you
choose to limit yourself when* everything
you seek is at your fingertips?

*Reflect upon your choices and the de-
tours they have resulted in. Learn from
your missteps and always remember to
choose the very best path. Do not sell yourself short. You deserve to travel the best
path. There are enough obstacles along the
way without deliberately choosing the
more difficult path. Set aside false pride at
taking the hard way and instead allow the
easy path to help you reach your destination with enough stamina to carry you
onward to the next leg of the journey. In
other words, stop making things so hard on
yourself!*

CHAPTER SIX

FINDING YOUR FOUNTAIN OF WORTH

The Akashic guides want you to know:

You are a magnificent soul temporarily housed in a third-dimensional body. You are perfection.

Self-love: Your Magnificence

We all wear masks to represent who we believe we should be to the world. From an early age we're taught to "put our best foot forward." Sometimes our disguises become so much a part of us that we believe they *are* our true selves. When you begin to see yourself through the distortion of a mask, it effectively cuts you off from Source energy, severely hampering your expansion.

That is a tragedy.

Source is another name for Creator (as in Source of all things). When you're energetically cut off from Source, you cease to thrive, like a flower deprived of sunlight.

You are unique, a grand creation, made to perfection. You are not broken, and nothing is wrong with you, so you do not need a mask. It's time to remove the mask and allow your authentic, beautiful self to be seen. The real magic in your life will begin once you open your eyes to the truth of who you are and start fully expressing your authentic being. The more often you connect with Source, the better.

Once you accept that you are a perfect, beautiful soul, new vistas will open for you, and you might even feel more love for yourself. You have worked hard to become who you are in this moment. Give yourself credit for how far you have come. Celebrate this accomplishment!

Does accepting your perfection mean that you can rest on your laurels and stop moving forward? Of course not! As long as you're breathing, you're meant to continue moving forward: growing, expanding, and evolving.

From the spiritual perspective, in each and every moment you are perfect and the moment is perfect for you. When you fully embody this truth, your life will be transformed. You'll experience fewer struggles and less resistance to what is. You'll discover an incredibly deep, inner peace in just being. Life will become exquisitely delicious.

That deliciousness is what you came to the planet to experience.

You Are Not Who You Think You Are

I'm going to go out on a limb here and assert that there is more to you than you've yet realized. Even if you love yourself. Even if you already meditate or do reiki. Even if you are known to be a wise and productive individual, there's still more. In reality, you're a beautiful, magnificent soul. So why doesn't it always feel like it?

Until my Akashic guides helped me understand this truth, I criticized myself mercilessly. Somehow, as a society, we've gone off track. There's an abundance of criticism, judgment, berating, and comparing ourselves to one another. When you think about it, it's amazing we get on as well as we do while under siege from ourselves and one another.

My guides have helped me gradually shift into a state of more love and less criticism. I'm a work in progress, as are we all, but I assure you this way feels so much better and opens the doors to creating a reality that is more satisfying and delicious than I ever thought was possible.

Yes, self-acceptance is possible!

Your Akashic guide team is steadfastly committed to helping you see the truth that you *are* a perfect soul. They are constantly broadcasting messages to help you recognize this truth so that you can find more joy and satisfaction than you ever imagined you could have. So that you will understand you deserve this and will progress on your journey to higher consciousness.

Your team is directly connected to the Creator, and they always speak divine truth. When they say you are perfect, you should believe them. After all, are you really going to argue with God?

I encourage you to stand tall in your beauty and power. Allow this truth to penetrate deeply into your being so that you never again forget who you truly are: a magnificent being capable of having, doing, and being whatever you want, with the help of a phenomenal spiritual team.

Your Metamorphosis

I know it's hard to accept the truth of your perfection. I've been there. But just sit with the thought of yourself as a magnificent soul for a while. Let it soak into your psyche. Try to wrap your brain around it and absorb it. Allow yourself to begin appreciating who and what you are just a little bit, and then a little bit more until you can embrace the powerful truth of your own magnificence.

Absolutely, strive to do more and be better, but understand that where, who, and what you are in each and every moment is always perfect for the moment.

You are enough. You were ALWAYS enough.

When you accept this truth, which is applicable to every human being, your life will expand in ways you cannot imagine. It won't happen all at once, but changes will unfold steadily as you walk the path of self-acceptance daily.

Right now, in this very moment, consider the idea that you become perfect in a slightly different way each day. (Heck, in each moment.)

Outside circumstances matter little. It's the inner you that counts. Work on aligning your ego and your higher self with your soul and everything in your life will fall into place in ways that feel far sweeter than you may have ever thought would be possible.

As I wrote this, I was given a visual to help illustrate the point. Think of yourself as a vessel. When you are in alignment, there is a straight line that runs from the Divine down into your soul, your higher consciousness, and your body—which is where the ego resides, energetically speaking. Due to this alignment of divine energy, love and light pours into you, filling your vessel.

Alignment is great. However, when you are out of alignment things get messy. Divine energy is still pouring in, but instead of filling your vessel it spills all over the place when it encounters the obstacle of misalignment. You are running at full speed while your energy tank reads as half empty.

This is why the topic of energetic alignment keeps coming up in readings, and will until we get it. Understand this truth at the depths of your being: Your Creator and guide team will never give up on you so please don't give up on yourself.

Your Authentic Self

What is your authentic self? That's the million-dollar question, right? How can you be your authentic self if you don't know what that means?

As you look around at the people you meet, you might think: *He knows who he is* or *She's really got it going on*. But outer appearances can be misleading. Most people are clueless about who and what they are at soul level. The soul, as it expresses itself through the person, creates the authentic self. Sure, people we admire may be managing well (and some quite well) without leading soul-centered lives, nevertheless misaligned people are not living up to their potential.

I've observed that some people have innately tuned in to parts of their souls and are using their gifts to some extent. A great many others, however, have no inkling of the full potential of their gifts. Some view their gifts as shortcomings, and criticize themselves for the very things that make them special and give them power. Can you believe it?

What people believe and how much of their divine gifts they are expressing has to do with how "awakened" their souls are. By that, I mean, the level of consciousness they have reached during their soul journeys thus far. Some are further along than others, and that is perfectly normal and okay. Where they are is perfect for them. Even "being asleep" is perfect.

Before you veer off track and start comparing yourself to others, and possibly find yourself wanting, let me assure you again that wherever you are is perfect for you. This is about *your* journey. In the here and now, you always have a new opportunity to expand your consciousness and take a giant leap forward.

That's what our current era with all its difficulties and planetary problems is largely about—taking a giant leap forward. Will you choose to keep treading the well-worn path, or will you seek a different path? One that's better suited to your unique gifts— your authentic self.

Enter the Law of Attraction

The Universe operates according to physical and metaphysical laws. One of these universal laws is that we create our reality through our thoughts (what you think about you bring about). Focusing on the positive helps you create more positive. Focus on the negative and you'll create more negative. You *are* the creator of your own reality.

If you're at all familiar with the movie *The Secret*, you may remember that it ends with the instruction "Feel good." That's the trigger to activate the law of attraction. It's not enough to merely focus on the positive, in order to manifest you also need to feel good, which results in less resistance thus opening the door for your positive manifestation to occur. Resistance is a natural result of being out of energetic alignment with your soul.

When you're feeling inspired to do something, such as to undertake a project or make a trip, but you're not sure of the right way to do it or whether to trust your concept, tune in to your inner compass—your solar plexus—and ask the question that needs to be asked. Then make the choice that feels best and *get moving*.

Inspired action is a signal to the Universe that you're engaged and ready. When you take inspired action without resistance, the most magnificent manifestations will flow in on the wave of your good feelings.

When you're in energetic alignment you will feel better, stronger, and more opportunities will come your way—far more easily than ever before. Each successful manifestation will in turn inspire more ideas and more manifestations.

Once the law of attraction has been set in motion, your life and the entire world will feel magical. The chain of events will be delicious and delightful.

Now, imagine stepping up your positive manifestations another notch on the dial. This is how the Akashic Records can be brought into the picture. Your personal records are a blueprint of your soul that hold every last, minute detail about the characteristics of your divine gifts. By reading the Akashic Records or having someone read them for you, you can hit the fast-forward button to success in any endeavor through retrieving that information.

Instead of guessing how your soul is wired, you can go directly to the Source and find out exactly what your strengths and potentials are. Armed with these insights, and by accessing your inner compass any time you have a choice or a decision to make, you can really shift life into high gear. You'll be unstoppable!

The Buried Treasure You Seek Is You

We tend to see the treasure we seek as something outside of us. However, after speaking with a great many Akashic guide teams on behalf of my clients, a common theme has emerged. According to these guides *we* are the treasure we seek. They think we're the be all, end all. And we *are* for them.

They encourage us to:

Drink deeply from the fountain of worth so that you can finally love and appreciate your magnificent self.

Read and contemplate the following five messages from the Akashic guides.

On Vision, Struggle, and Finding Your Door of Opportunity

Sometimes what you need and what you get are diametrically opposed. In those moments, it would be wise to take a step back, close your eyes, and focus upon each possible action you could take in turn. Feel your way through, searching for the soft spots. Those places that feel welcoming. Then gather those places, like pieces of a puzzle, and assemble a new picture. Create your own masterpiece by assembling the pieces that resonate. We assure you, the final result will be far more beautiful and satisfying than the original. This will be your own unique creation, and from it you will derive joy and satisfaction—perhaps with a healthy dose of profit as well.

Sometimes there is a tendency to get trapped within the confines of a once-created vision that no longer serves. If it's not working, it wasn't the right path, simple as that.

On Letting Go of the Past

Take a step back. Reassess. Reconnoiter. Take what works and discard the rest—you don't need it! Holding onto what was *in the hopes of burnishing it into the once shiny object of days gone by is an exercise in futility. It would be far better to spend your time looking forward, tweaking, testing, and implementing your newest brain child.*

Let go of the past. It is over. Take the lessons learned and draw strength from the wisdom gained. It will *serve you well.*

Put effort into making peace with situations you cannot change. They simply are, so try not to place judgment on them about good versus bad, just reach for acceptance. Peace lies in that direction.

On How Struggling Moves You Further from Your Goal

When you struggle against what is, or find yourself wailing about how bad it feels and how disappointing it all is, you are placing energy and focus on what you do not want. That would be fine if you wanted more of that. We presume this is not the case.

It would be wiser to accept what is and turn your eyes to focus upon what you intend to create next. Begin that forward movement and you will begin feeling better and better.

It is when you get stuck in this "feeling bad" space, mourning what might have been, grinding all of your efforts to a halt, that you will feel the most lost. Understand that this only perpetuates more of the same.

We say, have your moment of grief, then pick yourself up, focus upon that which you desire, and then take steps towards it. Baby steps are always fine. It is the act of moving forward that is vitally important.

Like winding a clock. As soon as you begin forward movement, the gears start turning and events are set into motion. This your guides can work with to help you reach that next "feeling better" place.

On Wailing in a Mud Puddle

When you choose to plop down in a mud puddle and wail, there is not much we can do. From that vantage point, you see clouds and rain, doom and gloom. Yet we tell you the sun is shining and glorious experiences await. When you decide to stand up and step out of the puddle, you will see the truth of what we say. It's always darkest before the dawn. That is poignantly true. Dawn always comes. It's a cycle. Believe it. Expect it.

Take the valuable lesson that you have learned and put it to use now to begin building up a head of steam to get your train back on track. You are the engineer and you are needed to drive this train forward into your destiny. Whether it be bright or dark is up to you. It's all a choice. If it were us, we know what we would choose.

Are you ready to reach for that which feels better? Today is a good day to begin.

On Moving Forward

One small step forward. Stop looking over your shoulder lest you be like Lot's wife. Place your focus firmly ahead. As you

*begin moving forward, you will feel better
and better. Keep reaching for more of that.
When it feels bad, reassess and change
course as necessary*

*You can certainly keep traveling in a
direction that does not feel good, but why
would you? What have you ever done so
wrong that you deserve to live in a state of
self-torture?*

*Nothing, we say! That is an illusion. Re-
ject that false notion.*

On Perceiving Yourself as Whole, Perfect, Brilliant, and Resplendent

*See yourself as your team sees you. Whole,
perfect, brilliant. Resplendent in your
magnificence. That is the truth of who you
are.*

*We urge you to wear your mantle of
brilliance for it is truth and will serve you
well.*

On Asking for Help from Your Akashic Team

Ask for our help and guidance. It is only a breath away. How much effort does a breath take? You see? It is not so impossible after all.

With all our love and encouragement you cannot fail unless you choose that path. It all comes back to choice. If you don't like your results, make a new choice, and another, and another, until you are at last fulfilled, happy and at peace. Go forth, be fruitful and leave your mark upon the world.

A treasure trove of valuable wisdom is sealed deep within your psyche. We urge you to tap into that power and embrace what once was. To call upon your inner guidance for strength and support. Know that we are always here, tethered to you like a lifeline, an unbreakable line. Centuries of experience and wisdom are cataloged and maintained for the day that you become aware and desire to tap into this resource. You need only ask and we will be at your side pointing the way.

You may not always recognize the signs, but we are persistent and will continue reaching out for as long as it takes. Look for signs and allow them to cast a light upon the dusty recesses of your memories. There are many resources at your disposal. We simply wanted to remind you of this, and urge you to call upon us always. We are your rock. We are your nuggets of knowledge. All safely stored for the day that you become aware and ask for our assistance.

Namasté.

CHAPTER SEVEN

KARMIC BAGGAGE

Reincarnation is intrinsically linked to the Akashic Records. In fact, it's the whole point. You Akashic guides have been tracking and cataloging your activities since your soul was created. That could be hundreds or even thousands of lifetimes for each of us. Kind of mind blowing, right?

Reincarnation

I once did a survey asking how many people believed in reincarnation. My expectation was that the majority did. Imagine my surprise when they didn't. The funny thing was that many more of them believed in reincarnation when it came to their pets. They reported being comforted by the idea that their beloved pets might come back to them, yet they didn't extend that idea to themselves.

I get it. There was a time when I thought reincarnation was a fantasy created by people afraid of death. I was convinced that we got one chance at life and needed to make the best of it. Part of my reasoning was that if (as I'd been taught), Christ died for our sins there was no need for us to keep coming back and atoning for previous wrongdoings.

I remember having a lively discussion with a colleague who was interested in such things when I was in my twenties. Older than I, he had concluded that, for him, reincarnation rang true. The memory is quite clear, which tells me that on some level I knew the truth of reincarnation, but wasn't yet ready to shift my beliefs to embrace it. My position changed over decades, as I became more comfortable with a great many ideas I had formerly dismissed as woo-woo.

What finally caused me to reconsider my long-held beliefs was science. If we're energy, as science has revealed, and energy never dies but only changes form, why would we stop with just one human experience? What else would we do throughout the eons of time? This idea planted a seed that slowly grew in my mind.

What caused that seed to finally sprout was *The Power of Myth*. In this series of six interviews between journalist Bill Moyers and mythologist Joseph Campbell that aired on television in 1988, Joseph Campbell aptly illustrates how the story of virgin birth was not original to Christianity, having shown up in other times and cultures predating the Christ story. That clinched it for me.

As I reflect on events, I now see that my journey to the Akashic Records began not long after the reincarnation conversation with my colleague.

My excellent therapist, whom I mentioned previously, was adept at using guided visualization as a form of treatment. During one of those visualizations I met a whale who guided me to an underwater cavern. There I found a set of stone stairs carved into the wall. They were carved on a curve so that they fit perfectly into the environment. At the top of the stairs, I found Jesus waiting for me. After he greeted me, he led me to a stone pillar, atop which lay a book that I understood was *The Book of Life*. I didn't know it at the time, but I had just been introduced to the Akashic Records.

I marvel at how spirit guide direction is so evident in retrospect—especially now that I know what to look for. I've come very far and shifted a great deal in my beliefs. I'm so different from the person I was. I consider myself to be at least Debbra 2.0, if not a more advanced model.

Readings and Past Lives

People often ask what is the difference between past-life regression and reading the Akashic Records. In my observation, it's a case of micro versus macro. A past-life regression is a microcosmic reading that focuses upon the specifics of one or more lives. This is where the reader is tapping into a past-life story or set of interrelated stories, if you will.

A reading of the Akashic Records is macrocosmic in that it includes every detail of your soul history and composition, including details of past lives if they are relevant to the question or concern that the reading is addressing. The purpose of an Akashic reading is not to learn the detailed story of a past life. It's more like perceiving vignettes encompassing a specific point or points in a life. The purpose often is to learn where a "glitch" may have occurred in the "software" that is having an impact upon you in the present.

Since you can't change the past, from the perspective of reading the records, there's no reason to go into great detail about it. The Akashic Records are an empowerment tool meant to help you with *present-life* issues.

As a reader, if I enter your Akashic Records, my intention is to receive the message your guides are sharing in that moment. This will always be what you need to hear right then. When it's time to deal with karmic baggage from a past life, your guide team will retrieve the relevant story. Once you understand the what and why, I can help you to energetically clear it, leaving you free of that issue going forward.

Unfinished Business

At least so far, everyone I've read for has had some past-life issues that were causing blocks and restrictions in their present-day lives. Some of these issues were minor, and a great many were major. It is common to have connections to people from past lives and to experience the karmic consequences of choices made during old lifetimes that need to be resolved.

The discovery of karmic baggage is subject to divine timing. Information about karma will only show up when you're ready to hear it and because it's something pertaining to the current situation that's under investigation.

Let me share a personal experience with you to illustrate *why* timing is important.

During a meditation, my most recent past-life incarnation was revealed. From the style of the cars I could see and other visual clues, I believe it was sometime in the mid-1940s or early 1950s. In that life, I was a woman married to a man who was insanely jealous, abusive, and controlling, who swore he would kill me rather than let me go. He beat me regularly, even while I was pregnant, with the tragic outcome that he killed our unborn child. Somehow that became my fault, and an excuse for him to give me more of the same treatment. The man tormented me for years, until I finally mustered the courage to plan an escape.

When my husband killed our baby in my past life, something inside me broke. The incident gave me the resolve to get out of his clutches as soon as possible. One cold, dark night, I slipped away, running for my life down a dimly lit street. A glimmer of hope alighted in my heart, warming me from the inside out. Relief at being free of his grasp spread over me. My pace slowed and I took some long, deep breaths.

Then I heard it. The sound of his old jalopy, roaring up behind me. Cold terror replaced the hope and warmth. I was momentarily frozen in place. He was close enough now that I could see his cruel face twisted in fury. A strange calm replaced the terror, and with it the acceptance of my fate. He viciously ran me down, killing me, just as he'd promised. Death was a welcome release. I was free.

You might be wondering why my guides would show me such a horrific memory. The reason was that I was ready to learn a lesson from it. I had paid the price for my unwise choice to marry an abuser. That left an energetic resonance upon my soul of victim energy—karma that would eventually need to be resolved.

During the first half of my current incarnation, I was a magnet for abuse. Victimization happened in a multitude of different ways. However, I did have a support system when I was growing up in the form of my amazing grandmother. She planted some "magic seeds" of love and wisdom that took root in me, ultimately leading me to recognize and step out of victimhood. Thanks to her support, I evolved into an empowered soul with the resources to successfully escape this negative energy pattern.

My guides knew it was important for me to see the through line of choices I'd made in that past life and how they impacted the woman I was then. This revelation helped me understand why I'd been drawn to my former husband in this lifetime: It was because we had unresolved karma. He was my abusive husband from that past life. By reconnecting with him in the present and successfully escaping the cycle of victimhood, I cleared the karma that had connected us.

Sometimes when you're inexplicably drawn to someone, it's because you have unresolved karma together. This may be particularly true of the most difficult people you know. Another mind-bending truth courtesy of the Akashic Records.

Did you just stop reading to mentally review the people in your life for possible karmic connections?

Mother/Daughter Karma

How many women do you know who have difficult relationships with their mothers? What if the reason is karmic baggage? A past-life connection that needs to be healed? If that's the case, the Akashic Records may be the best, most direct way to find healing and resolution of the issues and conflicts.

One story of karmic healing between mother and daughter stands out vividly. A woman, I'll call her Ann, came for an Akashic reading to help get through a challenging period in her life. As soon as I entered her records, I saw a visual image of a little girl cowering on the floor, hands protecting her face and head. An adult figure was standing over her, repeatedly stabbing her with a knife. It was a vicious attack!

Ann's tears began flowing when I described the image to her. She said it was her mother, who had always treated her like an enemy. She didn't treat the other children the same way, so young Ann was left wondering what was so wrong with her that her own mother couldn't love her? This was a betrayal at the deepest level, incredibly painful.

Slowly the pieces of Ann and her mother's story as souls connected in another lifetime began falling into place. They had been sisters in that past life. The mother was the older of the two. She was madly in love with a young man and desperately wanted to marry him. Unfortunately, he had eyes only for her younger sister (Ann). Social mores of the time dictated that the elder sister must marry first, so they were all caught up in what seemed an impossible, unhappy triangle. Older sister was jealous, petty, and vindictive. She couldn't bear that her little sister had outshone her. Much drama unfolded, eventually leading to the young man's death. Heartbroken, the older sister committed suicide. As you might imagine, this created a whole lot of karmic baggage that the souls of the two women would have to work out eventually.

For her current incarnation, Ann had chosen her mother for the explicit purpose of finding resolution of this karmic baggage. Instead, her mother seemed intent on continuing the vendetta, including through breaking up Ann's marriage. To compound matters, Ann's husband was the reincarnation of the young man they had both loved in the past life. Three souls were seeking resolution and failing miserably. Karma can be ugly, tangled, twisted, and mystifying.

Ann's mother was stuck in the old karmic pattern, most likely mystified by her behavior. Her attacks were not conscious. Ann felt betrayed and helpless. Without the insight of understanding, Ann would have carried the same karma forward to yet another lifetime.

The beautiful thing about seeking answers from your Akashic Records is that once you understand what the issue is, and why the issue exists, you're then freed up to change the dynamic by making new/different choices. Of course, Ann couldn't change her mother's behavior, but she was able and free to change the way she reacted to it. She chose to stop being tormented and victimized by her mother from that day forward.

Just imagine it. Something that tormented her for years was resolved in a very short span. With understanding came healing. Ann immediately began to feel better about herself, and to see her mother in a different light.

The amazing thing is that this karmic story was only a small part of what her guides had to share with her in that reading.

Are you getting an inkling of just how powerful and valuable a tool the Akashic Records are?

The Hiding of the Light Workers

There are a great many ultra-talented light workers on the planet, who are, for all intents and purposes, invisible to the greater part of the world. A light worker is a person who is energetically sensitive. They often practice some healing modality, whether formally or informally. Such an individual has a strong desire to make a positive difference in the world. Light workers toil valiantly with great heart and are beloved by those they've helped. You'd think that would translate automatically into success—that they'd have people waiting in line to work with them—yet it too often doesn't. Despite their earnest efforts to be seen, many live in obscurity.

I first experienced this phenomenon in the early 2000s, during a career switch from databases to working in equine rehabilitation. I experienced success bringing horses that had been labeled as hopelessly lame back to soundness. Due to what happened with me and my beloved horse, Misty, I became passionate about giving "throw-away" horses another chance at life and it was soul satisfying. However, despite my best efforts at marketing, I couldn't turn this healing endeavor into a profitable business. Many roadblocks showed up.

Finally, I gave up and began exploring other healing modalities because, not surprisingly, I needed an income.

When I finally discovered my soul purpose in the Akashic Records, I fully expected that at last I would easily build a profitable business while helping others. To my great surprise, similar roadblocks appeared. People raved about my readings. Lives were transformed. I was doing soul nourishing work. But people still weren't knocking down my door to have readings of their Akashic Records.

It simply made no sense to me. If I was living my soul purpose, shouldn't I be manifesting crowds of people who were eager to work with me?

Having hit those same roadblocks again, this time I dug in and began researching and analyzing, seeking an answer to this conundrum.

That's when I discovered that it wasn't just me. Blocks to prosperity and recognition were pervasive among light workers! Once I reached this place of awareness, I was ready to remove the karmic baggage interfering with my success. It was then that my guides revealed several past-life experiences where I had been a healer.

During the era of Salem witch trials, I was drowned on a dunking stool for my healing gifts. In another lifetime, I was a village healer.

Generations of villagers thrived under my care. Then, when I was quite an old woman, the traditions changed. I was no longer needed or appreciated.

There was a time when village healers were cherished, even revered. Then, as modern methods replaced old ways, they were shunned and scorned. In that lifetime, I was sent away to live out my days with only the company of a goat. It was a sad, cruel end to a life that had been devoted to caring for others.

In yet another incarnation, I dedicated myself to restoring fertility to a Bedouin sheik. I loved him and wanted him to be happy. When he finally began having children, he was grateful, but his appreciation didn't last long. Once his appetite for procreation had been satisfied, he had no more need of my services.

As I saw each of these lives, the riddle was unraveled. Healing others had resulted in being shunned, tormented, and even killed. The lesson my soul derived from these experiences was that it wasn't safe, or wise, to be a healer.

Studying the matter further, I learned that this pattern is common among light workers. Little wonder so many of us are effectively rendered invisible. It's about survival on an unconscious level! Light workers are out of energetic alignment with their soul purpose. In effect, they are actually manifesting invisibility.

Wow!

That was a big cookie to digest.

As usually happens, getting an Akashic answer instantly shifted my energy. Suddenly I became visible to the general public, and the manifestation doors opened. I began getting invitations for internet radio interviews. I overcame my lifelong aversion to the camera, and started making videos. I began speaking to groups. I experienced a powerful personal transformation. It was like a scene out of that old movie *The Jerk,* when the new phonebook came out and Steve Martin's character was elated to find his name included. He ran outdoors shouting, "The new phonebook's here! I'm somebody now!" It felt like after years of having an unlisted number, I was finally in the phone book. More opportunities presented themselves that ultimately led to writing this book.

Having thrown off the cloak of invisibility, there's important work to be done.

At one point during the journey to visibility my dog became very ill so I called out to my guides for assistance. It was then that Archangel Metatron made his first appearance. He gifted me with a healing meditation that concluded with the following message of hope and encouragement.

Relax and trust that all is as it should be. For it can be no other way. It must be so. Your time is now. It has arrived. Embrace it and revel in it. Make the most of the opportunities that have been given you and more will be given. It is a blessed day. Trust it, believe it, know it. For all the days unto eternity, this will be true. You need do nothing more than accept and allow it to unfold in your life, just as you asked.

CHAPTER EIGHT

RECOGNIZING MESSAGES FROM YOUR GUIDES

Isn't it peculiar that most of us are taught from a young age to ask a higher power, such as God or the angels, for help, and yet we're not taught how to recognize the messages we receive?

How to Recognize the Answers When They Come

It's not all that complicated to recognize answers to your prayers, but it does take some effort to learn. First, understand that answers *always* come when you ask. They have been coming all along. You just haven't always recognized them.

In my experience, they come in several different ways. An answer may come as:

An intuitive hit. It may come as a feeling of knowing in your solar plexus, or as hearing words in your mind. Sometimes you'll feel it, but then dismiss it because you think it's wishful thinking or your ego talking. *This couldn't really be the answer I've been looking for,* you tell yourself.

Now that you understand how intuitive hits come, tune in to your internal compass for validation when you think you're getting a message.

Numbers. Angels frequently use numbers to send us messages. You may notice that for several days in a row you wake up at exactly the same time, which is unusual. Or you'll observe that the same number starts showing up in your awareness. This may be a repeating number like 222 or 555, or something more seemingly random, like 1947. A message might show up in the numbers on the clock, in addresses, on license plates, or anywhere else, and you can know it is a message for you because it will be something that catches your attention. Very likely, you'll see it more than once in a relatively short period of time. Perhaps you've seen someone posting on social media about 1111. That number is an angel number about new beginnings, and a favorite among the metaphysical crowd.

The angels will keep sending messages, like a persistent telegraph, until you notice. When you do, stop and look up the symbolism. This is my favorite site for looking up numerical symbolism: SacredScribesAngelNumbers.blogspot.com.

Creatures. Depending upon where you live, animals may be a common way your guides communicate with you. I live in a rural area and I've had messages from all sorts of animals. Once a bald eagle swooped down in front of me on the road two days in a row. That was clearly a message, since I'd never seen this bird in real life until then.

Remember, an animal or bird message will be something out of the ordinary, used to catch your attention. Hawks are frequent messengers. But it can be any type of creature. Are you noticing a theme of being more conscious?

When a spider showed up in a reading, Olivia shared that she was having problems with spiders. They were everywhere, and she was quite distressed, as she had a great fear of them. In this case, her guides had probably been sending messages for quite some time without her noticing, so they stepped up their game to get her attention. Once she understood the message, spiders stopped being a problem.

Messages may be in the form of a dragonfly or a honeybee. I once had a butterfly land on my shoulder and pause for a bit. That was clearly a message, as it's quite out of the ordinary. The key to this is that it's some creature you hadn't really noticed before that suddenly shows up.

While driving into town one day, I encountered a skunk crossing the road in front of me. I'd never had that happen before. There had been lots of dead ones I'd seen on the side of the road, but never had a live one crossed in front of me, so I took notice. Then I got busy and forgot about it. My guides weren't going to let it go, however. Remember, they don't give up until the message is received.

Later that day, as I was traveling home, what do you think happened? Another skunk crossed in front of me! In fact, this one stopped in the middle of the road and stared at me. I had to come to a dead stop, because I was not going to go past that skunk. The skunk stood and stared at me in a way that was unmistakably a message. Then I got busy and forgot *again*.

You'd think I wouldn't. Happens to the best of us. Life can be distracting.

The next day, another skunk crossed my path. Three live skunks crossing my path in two days! Well, that was surely a message! This time I remembered, and when I got back to my computer I searched on Google to find out the symbolism of skunks. Just in case the number three was meaningful, I Googled that too. I won't go into all the details, but the skunk is symbolic of personal empowerment, which was meaningful at that time. Message received loud and clear.

Everyday objects. You know how after you get a new car you suddenly start seeing that same model, perhaps even in the same color, all over the place? It's like that with objects as messages. For instance, you might start seeing yellow cars and think to yourself, *That's funny, I don't remember seeing yellow cars before and now I'm seeing yellow cars all over the place. What is that about?*

Once you become aware of a specific type of object, repeat the same steps as you did with creatures or numbers. Stop, acknowledge that you've received a message, and then go to your favorite search engine to look up the symbolism. Check for yellow cars, the color yellow, or if you are seeing the same model all the time, look that up too. Whatever your object is, keep researching it until you hit upon a piece of information that resonates with you.

Sometimes the answer will be totally obvious from the start, other times it will be more obscure and you'll have to search harder and longer. This message might also be a bread crumb leading you toward a deeper message. Messages and symbols are frequently multilayered.

That probably sounds complicated, right? It can be sometimes; yet other times it is extremely simple. Just go with your instincts and trust that you're being led to an answer or message you need.

I promise, interpreting symbolic messages gets easier the more you do it. You can always ask for more clarification if you need it or seek outside help from an expert in these matters.

Your Assignment

Strive to live each day in a more conscious state. When you see something out of the ordinary, make a note of it; don't do what I did and forget. Put a note in your phone, leave a message on your voice mail, or write down your perception, doing whatever you must do to remember, because it's important. But trust that should you forget, the good news is your guides will keep bringing the bread crumbs to your attention until you get it because *they will never give up on you.*

This message came for a client who was desperately searching for her bread crumbs but not seeing any. Her spirit guide came in the guise of a shepherd out of the Old Testament. His name was Jeremiah.

You have missed your guide team doing cartwheels and jumping jacks trying to get your attention. With your focus on others, you could not see what was before you. Should you reach a space where no bread crumbs are in evidence, stop. Shut out the distractions and ask. Then trust the guidance that you receive. Many a time have we shared direction with you, but it went unheard or unused because you were unable to trust that it came from a positive, powerful place.

If you think you have received a message from your guides, you probably have. If it feels good, then try it. You will soon find out whether you were mistaken. Do this every time and eventually you will find that you have tuned the channel clearly enough that only true messages come through.

Who Are the Members of My Guide Team

The Akashic Records are overseen by Archangel Metatron. Under his direction, there are masters, teachers, angels, spirit guides, and enlightened beings. Most have been with you since your soul was created. Some you've added along the way.

You may also recruit additional help should the need arise. How cool is that?

Most of your team remain diligently working in the background. A smaller number work with you directly. It would be confusing and counter-productive for you to work directly with as many beings as are assigned to you.

If you ask, your guide team will identify themselves, however, they will also tell you that you're free to call them whatever you like. Names don't really matter in the fifth dimension, which is where the Akashic Records are housed.

Guides will often give names that have some meaning in your frame of reference. For instance, at the beginning of my work in the Akashic Records, several of my guides gave me biblical names (among them, Ezekiel, Isaiah, Elijah), as they were easing me into wrapping my mind around the vastness and intricacies of the Records and those were names I respected from my past biblical studies. As time passed, their names became more pedestrian.

Your guides may also take different forms, either due to symbolism or to amuse you or themselves. I told you about encountering Elissa, who appeared as the character Galadriel from the series of films based on J.R.R. Tolkien's book *The Lord of the Rings*. Most of the time, however, she comes to me in the form of a dragon.

Sometimes guides even change shape in the middle of a conversation. When I have asked why they choose a certain shape, they explained that sometimes it's for our entertainment, other times theirs. Some guides have a wicked sense of humor and delight in injecting mirth into interactions.

Does it surprise you to learn that angels and guides can be jokesters? Some people get quite offended by this idea. If you're one, let me assure you that in your case your team won't make jokes, because they know it would upset you. Many people are tickled when their guides display humor, so they show that side of themselves when appropriate. Since messages may often be quite heavy in nature, a bit of levity is welcomed. It is also a sort of reminder not to lose *your* sense of humor.

The following message came from the Akashic guides for a client who was seeking help with insight into a relationship. While her guides did somewhat address the question, they knew she needed a larger perspective and understanding as she has had more than her share of experience traveling through dark days. This is only a portion of what they shared.

> *Cycles of life always and forever spinning round. Ceaseless. You couldn't stop them if you tried. Wisdom gained—wisdom lost. Time ever marching forward. Always the*

taskmaster. Boom, boom goes the beat of the drum. Incessantly prodding. Pulling you forward like an invisible cord that draws you onward to the next experience and the next.

Sometimes it seems so pointless. Day after day of sameness, boredom, restlessness. Chafing at the constraints of society. Provoking thoughts of what is this all about? Is it really worth all the angst? What really IS the point of it all? When a boat merely bobbles in the water, never moving forward, or back for that matter, what IS the point?

Ah, my beautiful child, when you are consumed with such thoughts, the world can seem a pointless place indeed. However, there is a more encompassing perspective from which we assure you progress is real and tangible. Sometimes it feels as if all momentum has stopped. But in reality, you are moving forward, just in increments too small for your senses to measure. It is during these times when other events occurring outside your reality are bringing to culmination new possibilities from which you may choose.

When you feel impatient, please understand that your Akashic team is never idle.

Always and forever, we are making prep-arations to offer you new and exciting possibilities. Sometimes these prepara-tions take some length of time as people and events, and in fact their *choices, all must be calculated into bringing forth synchronicities for your perusal. While to you they may seem trivial, we assure you they are most definitely not. We can only lay the bread crumbs and wait to see which course you choose. Then adjust-ments must be made to align with the new present reality. There are many working parts!*

CHAPTER NINE

THE AKASHA AND THE LAW OF ATTRACTION

People frequently ask me, "How do I know whether I'm receiving a message from my guides or it's just my imagination?" The first thing to understand is that most people feel some doubt when they begin talking with their Akashic guides. With a little practice, they are able to differentiate easily. Eventually, most everyone can expect to reach a high degree of accuracy.

Learning to Trust Your Intuition

Intuition is an energetic muscle. The more you use it, the stronger and more accurate it gets. So, practice using it! Ask your Akashic guides to help you

133

attract small, easy things, like parking spaces, and expect them to manifest.

When I'm arriving somewhere that parking is likely to be dicey, I put in my request for a great space. It's a rarity that I don't find one waiting. Even then, sometimes by the time I park, another person will have pulled out of my perfect space. Had I waited, it would have been mine.

This is one of the easiest manifestations because we have little resistance to the idea of parking. Have fun with it.

Keep honing your intuition by asking, recognizing the answer, then acting upon it. The more often you're right, the easier it gets to trust that you really can discern a bona fide message from the voice of your ego. Practice and build your confidence so one day you won't even think about it, you'll just know.

Practice and Analyze

Exercise your manifesting muscle often. Set your intention, feel good, then send your request out to the Universe. Afterward, go about your day and don't worry about the how or when. That's the secret sauce to manifesting with ease.

When your intuition does get things wrong, pay careful attention. Analyze. What was different this time? Did it *feel* different?

Did you slip into thinking about what you didn't want?

Or maybe you spent too much time focusing on how hard it was to manifest something and fell into doubt?

Something will always be different when you get it wrong vs. when you get it right. Using *intention* and *paying attention* to detail, you'll soon find the pattern, and then you'll be in the driver's seat.

Once you're able to perceive the patterns of manifestation, you won't even be bothered by occasionally being wrong. It will feel wonderful to be empowered, and you'll be satisfyingly confident because you'll nearly always do it right.

Your Guides Always Act in Your Highest Interest

Your guides will never steer you toward something that would be bad for you. If you think you're being guided to do something that feels wrong, then it probably is wrong for you, but the advice is not coming from your guides.

Remember, earlier, how we talked about checking in with your internal compass? When you get what you think might be a message, check in. See how you feel.

Was your manifestation something you asked for, or something similar to what you asked for? For instance, did you ask for a long weekend, but an opportunity for a seven-day cruise came up?

When you are setting your intentions, and asking your intuition for guidance on how to manifest what you want, remember to utilize the concept of "this or something better." Say: "I would like a vacation/car/new boyfriend or something better." Let this become your norm when crafting affirmations or setting intentions.

One of the core principles of the law of attraction is that we need to remain open to receive in forms we might not have anticipated. The Universe is abundant and delights in giving to us. Your spirit guide team is like an intermediary that brings all the pieces together to assist in your magnificent manifestations.

We humans often can't see the bigger picture. Therefore, we need to allow our team to deliver something bigger and better than what we could imagine for ourselves. This might be something more suited to a grander vision for the new, more highly conscious you! By including space for something better, you're opening the door for the Universe to wow you with delight and amazement.

Should I Really Be Asking the Universe for Parking Spaces?

Some people might think it's inappropriate to be bothering the Universe with trivial things like parking spaces, but I can assure you there are a great many believers in this world who do it regularly and get great results. Apparently, the Universe is okay with it. People pray for all sorts of things. Asking the Universe, the Creator, the angels, your guides to help you manifest something you want *is* a type of praying. It's just a less formal way.

In reality, the Universe (and by extension, your guide team) is thrilled to be asked for help. We so often go it alone and neglect to reach out for help when we can. That's what they are there for. The spirit guides love to be asked. It allows them to more effectively do their jobs. Ask, ask, and ask some more. Don't worry about the how of things, as that's their job. Just ask, expect, and be open to receiving.

Allow yourself to receive. That is a key piece of the manifestation puzzle.

But beware of getting caught up in doubt or in fantasizing about reasons why what you want won't happen, or else you could manifest *that* unfavorable reality.

When I had my database business, I frequently told people, "I always have more business than I know what to do with." And it was always true. At the time I had no idea that I was manifesting these conditions through my words of affirmation. If I had, I likely would have changed the language to something more balanced. What I inadvertently manifested was too frenetic and stress inducing to be ideal.

When I became aware of the power of words, another light bulb went on. For years, I had been saying, "My metabolism is glacially slow." And guess what I manifested? Yup, a slow metabolism. Which meant I started putting on weight. You can bet that once I "got" this little nugget about speaking what you want I changed my language.

These days I often express gratitude for my amazing, high-speed metabolism that helps me to maintain my perfect weight. The reality of my physique hasn't quite caught up with my words yet, but I trust it will.

All the years of wrong belief form a powerful wall of resistance. That's okay. I'll keep chipping away at it with my new mantra and by thanking my body for being such a great partner.

I marvel at the incredible power of thoughts and words. If only I'd learned this earlier. Oh my gosh, what a difference it would have made! That's why it's so important for you, my friend, to absorb this concept and *deliberately* put it to work for yourself.

You are creating your reality daily through your words and thoughts. Do yourself a huge kindness and ensure that from here on forward you will speak and think in a conscious, deliberate manner. Then watch the magic unfold.

Manifesting on Steroids: Tweaking the Process

Once you've built your confidence not only to expect answers, but also to recognize them when they come, you'll be more aligned with your soul. From this place of alignment, manifesting can be as easy as breathing.

You may have heard people say, "What you think about you bring about." That's true. Once you're in alignment, you'll see that manifestation *will* happen more quickly.

It is ultra-important to watch your thoughts. For instance, if you have a bad day and get down on yourself, your mind may turn to negative thoughts like *That'll never happen, It's too much to ask, as those things never happen for me,* or something else along these lines. Guess what? If that's what you're thinking, then you'll manifest a whole lot of nothing, or worse something you *don't* want.

The Universe doesn't hear the word *don't*. When you assert what you *don't* want, it is as if you're putting in a request that you *do* want it, and since you have little resistance, it will manifest!

Start talking about what you want and leave the don'ts to the unenlightened.

The Timeline of Our Manifestations

Manifestations rarely happen on our timeline. There are bigger issues at play. Often, to deliver your request, a great many other pieces must fall into place. Since all humans have free choice, you could detour from your best-laid plans. When you do, your guide team needs to scramble to reset, re-align, and re-everything. We really keep them hopping, which is why each of us have a vast team. It takes a legion of Akashic guides to coordinate all the moving pieces of life and the world for their person.

Sometimes magic happens and a truly big thing will manifest rapidly. Those are sweet moments. And truly, sweet moments *can* happen even more often for you when you stay in alignment, set your intentions, and expect your miracle daily.

It's the absolute truth that a large manifestation takes the same amount of energy as a small one. Wild, right? In either case, manifesting requires the clearing away of limiting beliefs and your allowance to receive the desires of your heart.

You probably know someone who appears to lead a blessed life where everything just works out. That person has cleared their limiting beliefs and *expects* to receive what they ask for. No resistance = rapid manifestation. Life flows with ease and is so much sweeter in that place of delicious alignment.

Invite Someone to Co-Manifest with You

A biblical scripture that's frequently cited is Matthew 18:20-30: "For where two or three gather in my name, there am I with them." This passage means that the power of prayer is magnified when more souls focus their manifesting energy together.

Do you remember the *Ghostbusters* analogy I shared earlier? With more thoughts focused upon the outcome, the energy is strengthened through the belief of the collective. It's a powerful tool and may be just what you need to break through resistance and begin manifesting on steroids.

At the beginning of 2017, my husband, David, and I agreed to manifest a trip to Maui, Hawaii. We had been wishing and hoping for that trip for more than ten years. No amount of wishing or hoping had turned it into reality. Last year was a tremendous period of soul growth for me, as this was when I began receiving messages from Archangel Metatron.

When January rolled around, I was inspired to shift gears and focus on some co-manifesting. Understand that you cannot manifest *for* someone else, because that might interfere with their free choice. However, you *can* manifest *with* them! Even though I knew that David was in agreement with me about taking the trip, having him join me in consciously manifesting the trip felt like a worthwhile endeavor. Why hadn't I thought of that before?!

I shared my plan with him and asked if he would agree every morning to say aloud, "We're going to Maui!" with great enthusiasm. He was happy to play the game with me even though his spiritual beliefs are somewhat different from mine. The funny thing is that David was very motivated and proved to be much better at remembering to speak the affirmation aloud than I. He even sent me emails saying, "We're going to Maui!" or reiterating a variation of that intention.

In May, I discovered an opportunity to go to Maui that was better than I could have hoped. It brought several different manifestations together into a combined giant manifestation. Through co-manifesting with David, in five months we manifested what I had been unable to do in more than a decade. This book is a part of that manifestation and there is more to come. See what I mean? We can manifest bigger and better together!

Having achieved our dream goal, my husband and I are working on some other even larger manifestation—now being sure always to add the words *or something better* when we state our intentions aloud. It's an exciting way to live and feels wonderful. There's less resistance and more flow. Life is more delightful and adventurous this way. We feel like we're just getting started!

My Dear, You Had the Ability All Along

You are the captain of your (soul) ship. When you step into alignment with your soul, everything will change for you. When you can manifest as easily as breathing, it's more fun, less of a chore.

On one trip to the Akasha, I found myself in deep space watching a flock of mallard ducks fly by. The lesson/message that day was all about free choice, making our own decisions even in group situations. Remaining true to ourselves and our needs. Here is an excerpt of that message:

In one way or another you're playing your own game. With yourself and/or with others. Do you know what game you're playing? What defines a win or a success? Your choices. Did you know that? Your game, your rules.

You get to decide what a win is for you, so there's no need to compare yourself with others. They're playing a different game! Comparison is like mixing apples and oranges. There is no comparison— they are simply different fruits in the bowl. You are at the helm of your ship on this journey of life. YOU! Unless you cede your responsibility to others.

What you need to understand is that even if you have ceded control to another, you can also choose to take it back at any time! *It's always* your choice. *So, what will you choose for yourself?*

Can you see how it doesn't serve you to abdicate responsibility to anyone else? Others have different gifts, different ambitions, different goals than you. How then could their journeys serve yours? And make no mistake, if you cede control, you're choosing to go on someone else's journey, not your own.

This is also a choice.

We would ask you to consider how being on someone else's journey feels. Will you be content with taking their journey, or might you prefer your own unique one? Which would you enjoy more? And which do you suppose will lead you to higher consciousness quicker?

Your ultimate goal is to experience joy as you seek higher consciousness. It's about taking your journey of awakening.

It's time to awake, rise from your slumber, rise from your place on someone else's ship, and take the helm of your own vessel. Be the captain. That is what you intended when you chose this life.

If you look around and are filled with regret at missed opportunities, understand that it is never too late. So long as you are breathing, it's not too late. Make a new choice. Take a step toward the goals and dreams you have long held close to your breast. Now is your time. For if not now, when?

The Universe is inviting you to step into your destiny. To move toward the bright, shining, glorious future you've long envisioned. We tell you it is within your ability to create. All that is required is to lift up your eyes and focus them upon your own horizon, then step by step travel in that direction. For when you awaken to this truth, when you take inspired action, you will have at last stepped into your manifesting shoes.

Like Dorothy Gale in the land of OZ you always had the power, you just didn't know it.

That's the delicious truth of the Akashic Records. They contain all the answers as to the hows, whys, and wherefores all waiting for you to seek them out.

If you choose to sleepwalk through someone else's journey, you will never feel the deep satisfaction of your own accomplishments, and never feel deep in your being that you are living your purpose.

So, there you have it. Choices galore.

When you are ready to make your own choices a priority, shift gears out of Neutral and into Drive. We will step up our game accordingly to help you shift into Overdrive, if that is your desire.

Put us to work on your behalf. That is our purpose. We exist to serve and guide you! We await your choice.

We have all of eternity. Go forth and cast your bread (new choices), upon the waters and be amazed at what comes back

*to you. We wish you peace, joy, and love
for today and all your tomorrows.*

CHAPTER TEN

AKASHIC ALLEGORIES

When reading the Akashic Records, messages frequently come in the form of allegorical tales. I include a few here to demonstrate what this kind of reading is like.

A Visit to Oz

The doors to this archive are emerald green. They are shiny like the doors to the Emerald City in the L. Frank Baum book *The Wizard of Oz*. As I approach, the doors slowly swing open. Inside I see a yellow brick road with trees on either side and lots of vegetation. It's beautiful.

Now this is too weird. A bunch of munchkins come running up and grab my hands, saying, "Come on, follow us!" They lead me down the road and stop by the side where there stands a huge red tulip. It is magnificent. It bows and giggles as I approach. *"I am the emissary of the most high Lords of the Records. Welcome. What is your business here?"* the tulip says.

I explain that I have come seeking a message for one of my clients.

She ponders my statement for a moment. It feels as if she is communicating telepathically with someone. *"I see,"* she finally responds. *"Then a message you shall have."* With that she nods towards the Munchkins and they escort me further along the path.

"Thank you," I call back to her over my shoulder.

"De nada," she replies in Spanish.

It is apparently late in the day because the light is rapidly dwindling. The yellow brick road casts off light, and there are scattered lights here and there, but it is really getting too dark to safely continue. Just as I'm thinking that, the stars come out in all their majesty. The sky glitters with them like millions of tiny diamonds. *That's better,* I think.

Now, the moon has appeared. It's full and bright. Wonderful! Now I don't have to worry about tripping on a loose brick or whatever may be in the path ahead. The Munchkins are singing, *"Follow the yellow brick road."* We are *definitely* not in Kansas!

I realize the Munchkins are leading me to the Emerald Palace. We're going up the steps. The guards step aside to allow us entrance.

We're now inside and it's beautiful, just like you see in the movie. They take me right into the throne room. There are mirrors and some smoke and gauzy green curtains. It's quite a display. Then out from behind the curtain appears the Wizard. He has been outed so no longer feels the need to put on a big show for visitors.

The Wizard kindly greets me and invites me to sit and have tea. *"So, you have come seeking a message?"* he inquires.

I nod affirmatively.

That is splendid. We would very much like to send our highest regards and admiration. Your friend is something of a legend in these parts. Long ago when she was but a wee bairn (he winks), *she set upon a path to bring love and light into the world. It has not been an easy path and there were many U-turns and missteps along the way. She has had to change and adapt immensely to stay afloat in some pretty stormy seas. To be honest, she really expected to be further along in her endeavors by this point in her life. But she should understand that events have played out as they should. Nothing is wrong and the phrase* should have *needs to be stricken from her vocabulary.*

Self-recrimination is a poisonous fruit. It causes doubt and shakes her self-confidence. It is a trap sprung upon the unsuspecting by their egos. A trap that stops progress dead in its tracks. Life is about taking risks. Sometimes you succeed, sometimes you fail. The ultimate failure is to stop trying. No matter how overwhelming things get, she needs to stop, regroup, take a deep breath, and then begin again. One foot in front of the other, just like a baby learning to walk. Notice how babies never give up despite the bumps and bruises? They are indomitable, and so should she be.

We say to her, "Let your passion spark a fire in your belly that feeds and motivates. Always be on the lookout for new ways of accomplishing goals. Strive to learn something new every day. Keep your mind sharp. You have only just begun to tap into your potential. Turn the volume down on the speakers when those voices plague you with recriminations and mock your efforts. Remember that is your ego trying to keep you in a safe, familiar place. Kick it to the curb and show it who's in charge. You are the powerful creator of your own destiny. Embrace it with all your passion and creativity and watch your soul bloom like the red tulip who greeted you earlier.

"Is there anything else you would like to share?" I ask.

There's no rush. Allow events to play out as they need. Trying to control things that are not within your ability to control is an exercise in futility. It's also a colossal waste of time. That time would better be spent on things that bring you joy. Follow your bliss *is more than a catchphrase. It is truth. That is exactly what she had in mind when she began this journey. She had lofty plans and was on fire with a desire to change the world.*

Tell her there is still plenty of time to do so. Just to remember there's no rush, she has plenty of time, and when it does run out she will get to do it all over again. She can't fail and it will never be complete. The idea is to move closer to the goal and she has done that quite well.

Please remember to laugh often and keep the spark of childlike wonder alive. At your core that is who you will always be, a child filled with wonder and delight. Do not allow expectations of others to derail your plans. It is up to you how you spend your time and in what activities you partake. That is plenty for now. We bid you both adieu.

The Twilight Zone?

The doors of this archive were lemon yellow with silver sparkles (like twinkling stars) scattered over them. The color was so vivid I could almost taste lemon.

As the doors opened, I could see a vista of green grass spreading out in front of me, seemingly going to the horizon. It was beautifully manicured, absolute perfection, you could say, not a blade of grass out of place. The sky was a pale blue and there was not a single cloud. It was bright and inviting.

Off to my right, I noticed movement. I turned to see what it was and spotted a large snail crawling along. It turned to look at me, smiled, and winked in acknowledgment of my presence, then continued its journey.

Just then, I heard a loud bird call and saw a bald eagle swoop down upon the snail, grabbing it in its talons then fly off. As the eagle connected with the snail, the eagle looked me right in the eye and sent me the thought that this was as it should be. "*It's the way of the world; the weak make way for the strong.*"

I watched as the eagle flew off into the distance, finally disappearing. I was thinking that the eagle apparently had a taste for escargot. *Maybe he was French?*

A beautiful, orange monarch butterfly flitted across my path. It was flying loop de loops, simply celebrating life. It had such evident joie de vivre. It flew off to my right and was soon gone from sight.

A big, fluffy cloud rolled in from the left. The wind was picking up and now more clouds, some quite dark, had arrived. The temperature had dropped, the wind was really whipping, at least thirty-five miles per hour, and it was beginning to rain. First, just a few drops, then it began really pouring, pelting me in a punishing manner. I looked around for shelter and noticed a Hobbit-like house built into a hill. Its roof was grass so it was camouflaged from view until I needed it.

I ran over to the little house and knocked on the door. There was a light in the window casting a warm glow into the stormy outdoors. After what seemed like a very long time, but was truly only moments, an elderly woman answered the door. She was thin and slightly stooped over, less than five-foot tall, with white hair and round, silver, spectacles perched on her nose. *"Yes,"* she said, *"how can I help you?"*

I quickly explained that I was caught in this storm, unprepared, and wondered if she would perhaps offer me temporary shelter.

"Of course, I'm so sorry, please come in," she said as she opened the door wider.

I stepped inside and stopped at the door so as not to drip water all over her home. She said, *"Wait just a minute, I'll get you a towel."*

A moment later the old lady came back with a big, fluffy, dark brown towel. It was quite luxurious and absorbent. I was feeling much better already. She took the wet towel from me and offered me a robe in the same luxurious dark brown fabric. It was like terry cloth, but much softer and with more density.

I took off my wet shoes and socks and found a pair of matching slippers that I gratefully put on.

"There, that's much better," she remarked. *"Come, let's get you something warm to drink. How about a nice hot toddy? That will warm you up and help prevent a cold."*

I'm not normally a drinker, but there was something about her presence that compelled me to say yes. I took the steaming mug from her and sipped it slowly. The beverage had a marvelous butterscotch undertone that reminded me of Ronrico Rum.

Once I had dried off and was warming up, I noticed that her kitchen table was one of those 1950s-style tables that are considered retro. Her home was well kept, everything in its place, and it exuded coziness. It occurred to me that I had not introduced myself or asked her name. "Pardon me for my lack of manners," I said apologetically, then told her my name and inquired about hers.

"That's quite all right," she said with a smile. *"I'm very pleased to meet you. My name is Annabelle."*

I stifled the urge to laugh as that name did not seem to fit her at all. Maybe Miriam, but Annabelle? Then I got a flash of vision showing me what she had looked like as a young woman. She was quite a beauty and a little taller than now. It was an abrupt message about not judging a book by its cover.

Her eyes were twinkling as if she had just read my thoughts. I blushed with embarrassment. She put her hand over mine and very kindly said, *"Shush, no need. If a person lives long enough they will experience all manner of transformations. It's the way of the world."*

For just a moment, I wondered whether she was the eagle I had previously seen. *Could she be a shapeshifter?*

Again, she appeared to have read my thoughts. She shook her head and giggled, then said, *"No, I'm not a shapeshifter, although I wouldn't mind being able to fly. It's just a shared truth of man and beast."*

A moment later, I was standing back out on the green carpet of grass and the sun was shining. I didn't even get to thank Annabelle for her hospitality; it was as if I blinked my eyes and was transported back there. The Hobbit house was no longer visible. It had all happened so fast I wondered if it was real. (A bizarre thought, considering where I was to begin.)

As I looked around in confusion, a frog came hopping up. It had cartoonish proportions and as it got closer I could see that it was the size of a cow. It was wearing a bowler hat and tipped the hat at me as it settled down directly in front of me. It had blue eyes and the appearance of a person inside of a frog. If I tilted my head I could see a man, and yet it was a frog. Like one of those holographic pictures that changes depending on how you hold it. Stranger and stranger.

"Howdy," he finally said. *"Buck Rogers at your service."* I had to stifle a chuckle at that.

"Hi, Buck," I answered. "I must say I am very confused by what I have seen today. Can you help me to understand what's going on?"

"Why sure, little missy. You've entered the Twilight Zone," he paused for effect. (Now I was really confused.) Then Buck Rogers delivered the following message.

Naw, I'm just pulling your leg. The Twilight Zone *is fiction! Truth in these parts is much better than any fiction. So, you want to know what's going on? Okay, let me explain it to you. Sometimes folks have a hard time understanding why certain things happen "to" them. They worry and fret, fuss, and fume, spinning their wheels in a mighty big way all because they can make no sense out of their lives.*

I'm here to tell you that there is a rhyme and reason to everything under the sun. Actions and consequences. That's the crux of it. Sometimes those actions happen at a level of near unconsciousness so that a body has no recollection of them. No matter. Once a stone is set to rolling down a hill, it will gain momentum swiftly, and then anything or anybody in its path better move if they know what's good for them.

Sometimes life feels like a runaway freight train. That momentum thing can be a real bummer. But you need to understand that you are in control of events. It is your choice whether to set that stone to rolling. If you pick a different action, the consequences will be different. Cause and effect, you see?

Strive to live in a conscious manner so that you don't inadvertently set events in motion that end up with you feeling like a splat on the pavement. Live consciously, get it? Be responsible for your actions. Step up and make better choices and you'll have better consequences.

Do not rush into things. Take the time to carefully contemplate whether the risk is worth the reward or the punishment, as the case may be. Act in haste and live in regret. Slow down, you have plenty of time.

Think about the chain reaction before you set things in motion. It just might be that with a simple step to the left or right you'd discover a much better outcome. Remember that rolling stone? What if someone (like you), placed a smaller stone in its path that caused a change in trajectory? Perhaps the new trajectory took that stone down a path where it plugged a hole in a dam. Now wouldn't that be something to celebrate? Cause/effect, actions/consequences. That's all we want you to understand.

Live in a conscious manner and you will soon find that you get more satisfying outcomes. You have a beautiful, marvelous brain and we want you to take full advantage of it. Get those cells firing on all cylinders. Make it work for you. Allow your creativity to burst forth and produce beautiful bouquets of wonderfulness. You have it in you to create show-stopping moments so magnificent that you will stand in awe of them.

What are you waiting for, an engraved invitation? Yes? Well, consider it delivered. We hereby invite you to step into your power and create the best version of you that ever existed. So, it is and so it will be.

So say we all.
Amen!

Birthday Celebration 2014

The doors of my Akashic Records open inward on this day, whereas normally they open outward. As

I step through them, I see white light with red flowers popping up. I can't make out what they are. They pop in such a way as to look like droplets of blood. Then there are some yellow flowers as well. Blues join in. Green next appears. Then orange and purple.

The entire set of chakras is represented by these colors. It is like a field of colorful flowers without grass. Stark whiteness is all around me, and black droplets are coming down as if dripping down a wall, leaving a streak behind. Black streaks here and there obscure part of the image of the lovely flowers.

Now rain. I can see translucent rain drops. They are blurring all the flowers. The entire scene morphs into a watercolor with the rain diluting the colors. Colors are running off and leaving behind streaks in varying shades of each color.

Then the sun comes out. It shines brightly, looking like a picture of itself, with spikes. It feels as if I am in a children's picture book.

Two-dimensional characters begin approaching. Cartoonish-looking children and a brown pony. The pony speaks in a self-deprecating manner. Then they move along, seemingly not at all interested in my presence.

I look around to see what else they will offer me on my special day. "Hellooooo," I call. "It's my birthday. Is there no one to talk to me?"

With that, it was as if a surprise party was being held. Birds come flying into the scene holding gifts in their beaks. Animals approach. The archangels float down. They are all beaming with a delight that surprises me. I get hugs all around, even from the wiggly puppies and the purring cats.

An older man with a gray beard, he's the prophet Isaiah from the Old Testament of the Bible, steps up and says, *"You didn't think we'd forget?"*

"I wasn't sure what to expect," I confess.

"We wouldn't overlook your special day. It is sacred here in the records. Each birthday in each life is a sacred date and not to be forgotten. The birth date makes an indelible mark and then a new series of records begin at that point. Those are major markers in the archive.

"On this occasion we thought it was appropriate to discuss the direction of your journey," he explains.

"I would like that," I reply.

Isaiah continues, *"Your life has taken many unexpected twists and turns. It has taken you quite some time to arrive at a place of enlightenment. We wish it had happened sooner, but nevertheless it* has *happened and we will make the most of it. There is much catching up to do. That is why life seems to be moving past at such a frenetic pace. You are racing to catch up with the timeline that you had planned. It is entirely doable so you need not worry that you arrived too late to the party. Everything is as it should be."*

He chuckles. Then says: *"Come, let us walk together."*

Isaiah leads me away from the festivities to a quiet grove of trees where we sit on the grass and talk. I am aware that he intends to thoroughly ground me for our conversation. I can feel a firm attachment to Earth as if I am tethered in place. It is a very stable feeling, secure and yet not trapped. I am free to move as I wish despite my tether.

"Are you comfortable?" he asks.

"Quite," I respond.

"Good, now let us continue. As I was saying, you are right where you are supposed to be at this moment in time. Do not waste even a minute thinking otherwise. From this vantage point, you are poised to accelerate into the destiny that has awaited you. It will be a marvelous ride. But hold on to your hat as there will *be some bumps. Nothing you cannot handle, surely, but expect some bumps for they make things more interesting. It's all about how you handle the bumps that affects their resolution. Some you will sail through, others will bog you down.*

"No matter, as you will quickly find your way beyond the speed bumps and get right back on

track. You have built up a head of steam and are nearly unstoppable.

"Don't forget to enjoy the journey. The tendency is to get caught window gazing rather than participating. That would be unfortunate as you would rob yourself of the exquisite depth of experience to be had.

"When life feels too much like a runaway carousel, remember that you can get off and catch your breath. You are in control, not events. If you keep that bit of wisdom in mind you are less likely to be overwhelmed when events conspire to run you off the track."

With the message concluded, Isaiah stands up and we walk back to the party. It is loud and over stimulating and I elect to bow out. They apparently did not need my physical presence to party. Happy birthday to me!

CHAPTER ELEVEN

FREQUENTLY ASKED QUESTIONS

As we're nearing the end of the book, I thought it would be helpful to share examples of typical questions my clients ask during readings of their records and the answers they receive from the guides. It should help you get a flavor for the wisdom of the Akasha and the range of personalities among guide teams. Questions can be about anything. However, it is common for people to ask about money, relationships, and spirituality.

Q: Can my Akashic guides offer any insight upon my spiritual journey? Am I

on track? What do I need to tweak? What else can they share with me?

We say you are a wise person for seeking assistance with that which you desire. Being open to messages and signs from your team is a powerful tool that will carry you far on your journey.

When you are unsure, rinse and repeat. Always we stand by ready to give assistance. Watch for answers in your daily life. Listen to that feeling in your gut. Follow your internal guidance system. You will know you are on the right path because it will feel so good. If it does not . . . well then, you have your answer. Time to course correct.

You have everything you need to find success. Believe in yourself. Take your time—no need to rush. Allow events to unfold as they will. Take advantage of opportunities that arise. You see? It's really a simple recipe. You already possess everything you need, plus with our help how can you not succeed? Now go out there and get it done! We'll be here waiting should you have more questions. Peace and love.

Q: How can I get to a higher spiritual level before my life ends?

By living, baby! Get out there and live! Relish the days for they pass all too quickly. Find what gives you that buzz of euphoria and do it, do it, do it! Do not make it more complicated than it is. Life is truly quite simple. Live, expand, experience your wonderful, creative, incredible self! Rinse and repeat at ever-increasing levels. It's like driving up a winding mountain road. One level at a time until you reach the top and then enjoy the view! Voila.

Q: How can I clear what feels to be negative karma, so that I call toward me the level of prosperity that is truly for my best and highest good?

Dearest, we see you struggle and it pains us. It is as if you are stuck in a pit of quicksand. Try as you might, you cannot free yourself. May we point out that while you were struggling we dropped a rope down so that you might extricate yourself? All you need do is center yourself. Breathe. Relax. Stop struggling and look for the way out we have provided. It was there all along. You were just unable to see it due to your distress. Trust, sweetheart. We will never abandon you. Close your eyes and allow your senses, your intuition, your inner guidance to direct you to the exit. We've even given you more than one so that you may choose the one that is most convenient.

Just as when you are swimming, if you relax and gently tread water you will float. If you panic and struggle you will not. This is a huge trust issue for you. You have forgotten that you can trust us implicitly. You doubt us, you doubt yourself, you doubt the future.

Snap out of it! Breathe. Center yourself. Relax. Meditate. Trust! *Look for the guidance that is dangling right over your head. When you see it, act upon it. If you hesitate and miss the opportunity, never fear. We will present another and another until you do see and act upon it. We will* never *desert you. We cannot desert you. Our entire reason for being is to guide and support you. Your success is our success. We're a team, get it?*

C'mon girl, we've got this. Are you ready to get the party started? Let's make like a bee and buzz. It's groovy baby. Come on in, the water's fine.

The message ends to the tune of "La Bamba."

Q: I battled to get my son into rehab and now he hates and blames me for his addiction. I have only been good to him, fighting for him when no one else cared. Yes, I made mistakes, but I also

dedicated myself to him. How do I deal with his hatred?

Precious, we have seen how you fought for your son. You were valiant, his gladiator. Often in such situations, the gladiator feels the wrath of the one they fought to save. When people are not ready to take responsibility for their own choices, they must place the blame elsewhere. Your son recognizes that it is safe to rail and rage at you because you have already demonstrated you won't give up on him.

What you can do right now is take care of yourself. Do not accept the rage and all the negative energy. It is not yours. Love him, support him, but do not allow him to abuse you emotionally. That would not serve either one of you. He is still recovering. Whether he completes the process and takes responsibility is totally up to him. This is something you cannot do for him. Once you can block his wrath, he will have to take new action as blaming you will make him extremely uncomfortable.

Please understand, this issue of addiction is not about any mistakes you might have made in his rearing. All parents make mistakes. No more blame-game for you, is our prescription. Time to love and appreciate yourself for the warm, loving, caring woman that you are. Give a little of that love and caring to yourself. Fill your heart with self-appreciation.

Stand secure in the knowledge that your sacrifice and battle for your beloved son have not gone unnoticed. Whether your son is ever able to acknowledge the wrong he has done you and apologize, we see and appreciate your strength. We acknowledge the warrior mother. We send you accolades. Please allow our love and appreciation to flow into your being and heal the wounds.

You are so very loved on this side of the realm. We will always stand steadfastly in your corner. Please avail yourself of our assistance wherever and whenever the need arises. We are your team. Boo yah.

Q: Please share with me how I can hear and attune myself to the messages of my guides.

I'm shown a visual of taking the lens cap off a camera. Then they say:

You DO hear them, but through a filter. When we speak you often hear, but you have not been able to trust that it is your guides rather than your imagination.

You must remove the trust filter. It isn't necessary. Simply accept what you hear, and believe it to be true. Sometimes it will and sometimes it won't. That's your learning curve. You must trust, take at face value what we say even though sometimes it feels ridiculous. Sometimes we are ridiculous to make a point. Do not judge what you hear, see, and feel. Accept. Allow. As you begin to take tentative steps towards trust you will notice the spigot opens wider and wider until it flows freely.

Trust, my dear. All you must do is trust. Take baby steps. Rome wasn't conquered in a day. Likewise, this will take time. When you get it wrong, take note. Did that time feel different? Was there an off feeling? Contrast and compare until you no longer question the guidance you receive. One day you will notice that you get it right more than not.

Practice. Practice. Practice. It's a beautiful thing.

This last comment was said in a singsong voice while I got a visual of the guide who was speaking dancing around. The image was a blur, but the guide looked a bit like Snoopy from *Peanuts*.

The guide continued:

What's more, be patient with yourself. Put away the critical judgment and accusations of being less than perfect. See yourself as we see you. Glowing with the light of the divine. Glowing with positive intentions. Yearning to make a difference in the world. If you had a friend who looked like that what would you tell her? Would you say she wasn't good enough or would you marvel at how exquisitely she expressed her divinity? If you'd do that for a friend why not for yourself? You see? Lack of self-acceptance is at the bottom of more human problems than any other thing. If you could only remember who you truly are.

Boom boom boom [the sound of a bass drum] *We're here to remind you.*

Then I heard Dionne Warwick singing *"I'll Never Fall in Love Again,"* and the guide said:

Now, that's a lesson in negative law of attraction! Look at those lyrics and rewrite them in positive law of attraction speak. See if any revelations pop up. That's all.

Toot toot [I heard a sound like a toy train].

Q: I've struggled with some difficult health issues. Is this the year I finally get my health back?

I'm seeing/hearing static. Like a radio between stations. It's clicking back and forth trying to find the right frequency. It comes in for a bit then goes out again. There's something blocking the signal. Then I hear whistling, like a short-wave radio is being tuned. A lot of effort is going into finding the perfect frequency, but there is a misalignment, so a connection cannot be made. A feeling of frustration. Take a step back. Let's take the long view and get some perspective.

Wow, the long view bounced me right into outer space. Ah, a satellite. Perhaps the power of a satellite will bring clarity? Yes, I can hear fragments of speech. Still not clear enough to understand what is being said. More of those high-pitched whistles. Perhaps some fine tuning of the satellite is in order?

Oh, I just got it. We are waiting for the planets to align. It's like night and day alignment, if that makes sense. *When the Earth revolves around to align just so, the satellite will provide a strong signal and the voices will come through loud and clear. Until that alignment occurs, it is an exercise in futility to try to force it. You can strain your ears, use amplifiers, headphones, and all manner of other gadgets, but you won't be able to reach clarity until the planets align. This is bigger than your desire. There are components that are out of your control.*

Now I see a long tunnel with a bright, shining light at the end of it. That is hope.

You will find your way out of the darkness, but you will need patience and perseverance to get there. Know that what you desire is available to you. Trust that you will get there. It will not be easy, and may even be painful, but if that is your desire you will ultimately prevail.

One step at a time. Keep your eyes on the prize. It will be exhausting. At times it will be exasperating, and you will have days where you don't want to get out of bed. But maintain your focus on the desired result and it is possible. You cannot force it.

You must remain steadfast, doing your part, and allow the healing to occur as you reach alignment. Then, oh baby, it will be glorious! That which you have wished for, worked for, sweated for, and bled for is at hand. It is in the realm of possibility.

It won't be a picnic darlin', but you are one tough cookie and you have what it takes to make it so. May sunshine and roses surround you in your darkest hour and bring you peace. Selah.

Q: What message do my spirit guides have for me today?

We are so delighted you asked.

I see the image of a big grin and I hear the song "You've Got a Friend," which then switches to "You've Got a Friend in Me." Then a guide speaks.

It's an excellent time for introspection and reflection. What can we help you with in the new year? We will. Just ask. Oh, baby, don't hesitate, that's what we're here for. No trouble at all.

Aww, we're just playing with you. We want you to know how eager we are to be of service. Seriously, doll, when we're not helping you we're just twiddling our thumbs and that gets real boring after a while. Give us something to do. We are ready, willing, and able.

All kidding aside, we really do want to help. You've got big plans and we've got big hands. Heavy lifting is our specialty. No job too big or small. Come on, let's play ball.

Now I'm hearing the Beach Boys singing "Barbara Ann" followed by "Da Do Run Run." The reading was turning out to be a regular concert!

What? Us be serious? Why? Whatever for? She likes it this way. She's a girl that knows how to enjoy life and we appreciate that about her. We just wanted to be sure she knew that. We can have lots of fun and big adventures together. Let's rock and roll!"

You said any messages would be welcome. We can be serious another time. Tonight, we wanted to show you a good time. You deserve it. We love, love, love you.

CHAPTER TWELVE

Connecting with Your Higher Consciousness

From time to time when I visit the Akashic Records, my guides will share a meditation. Whether the purpose is to create general well-being, undergo healing, manage grief, establish a deeper connection, or something entirely different, each meditation is profound and beautiful, and crafted with care to have the maximum impact. The meditation in this chapter is no exception. The Akashic guides wanted to share an extra special experiential process with you, and this guided visualization is what they created.

As a gift, I've recorded an audio version of this meditation for you so that you can simply sit back and allow the experience to unfold. You can download the audio file for free on my website. (See the *Resources* section of this book for that link.)

If you're like me, the first time you listen to a meditation you may get distracted by wondering what's coming next, or in this case, by trying to decide upon the details of your surroundings. To bypass distraction, I decided to give you an opportunity to read through the meditation first so that when you listen to the audio you will be fully relaxed, getting the full benefit of the experience.

So, without further ado . . .

A Meditation to Reset Your Soul's Default Settings

Select a quiet comfortable space where you'll be uninterrupted for half an hour or so. Then, sit back, close your eyes, and begin by taking three deep, deliberate breaths. With each exhalation, release any tension you're holding in your body.

Now, continue breathing normally. Focus on your breathing as any tension slips down your neck, into your chest, past your abdomen, and into your lower body. Slowly and steadily, the tension moves down, and still further down, until finally it exits through your feet and toes, leaving you feeling so relaxed that your body feels as if it could melt into a gentle pool of water.

With your eyes still closed, picture yourself in your very favorite place. Slowly look around and take note of your surroundings. How does it make you feel?

Is this a place of peace and tranquility? If it's not, feel free to shift the scene to one that is. You get to set the scene. You are an artist painting a picture that need only satisfy you. This is your personal oasis. Your refuge. Your sanctuary. Add colors, objects, plants, animals, whatever you need to create *your* idyllic space.

Take a moment and create your most perfect, sacred space. Visualize that you are lighting a candle, burning incense, diffusing essential oils, or doing whatever else you would like to make the scene a feast for your senses.

Once your creation is complete, spend a few moments just absorbing the peace and tranquility of it. Allow yourself to slip deeper and deeper into a state of total relaxation.

In your scene, are you sitting, standing, or lying down? What is the surface you are resting upon? What is your body position?

You are about to do important work, life-changing work. So, whatever it takes in order to bring full focus to your time here, that is what you need do.

If you find your mind wandering during the meditation, bring your focus to your breathing.

Don't worry about anything else. All you need do is breathe and allow the scene to unfold.

Take your time to set the stage and you will set yourself up for success.

Now we begin.

When you're ready, use the breathing exercise you previously practiced as you return to your idyllic place. Get comfortable and soak up the soothing ambience of your creation. Notice and appreciate the details.

Now allow yourself to consider the life path you're currently on. Observe only the good parts of your life. For the moment, let there be nothing else in your world, only that which serves you and feels good.

Notice that as you focus upon the juiciest, most delicious parts of your life in your visualization, they begin to expand. They are increasing right before your eyes, taking up more and more space in your reality.

Let these pieces continue their expansion, adding even more delightful pieces. Good begets more good, acting like a magnet, attracting more beauty, love, and abundance to you. Notice how easily it's unfolding in your reality. The only effort you need make is relaxing, breathing, observing, and appreciating.

How do you feel? Would you like to feel this way more often? Your guides assure you that you can. Your visualization is your creation, your reality. And you have the same ability to create a new version of reality whenever you like—even when your eyes are open. Practice until you can make changes in seconds.

The more you focus upon the idyllic version of your life, the faster your personal energetic frequency will shift. That will bring you closer into alignment with your soul, making you a magnet for that which you desire.

Later, as you go about your days and feel inspired to take new action, don't hesitate. Move forward taking more and more inspired actions. Inspired feelings are like bread crumbs leading you toward the opportunities that will allow you to turn your inner vision into concrete reality. Yes, there are moving parts, but as you can see in this visualization, they are not at all difficult to move around energetically. Matter follows energy. If you are willing to put in the time and effort, your dreams can become reality.

Continue focusing on your breathing and allow this new way of thinking and your new vision for your life to permeate your being. Feel it reprogramming your energetic circuits to attract, rather than repel that which you want. Do you see how effortless it can be?

Take a couple of deep breaths. Just *be* for a moment.

Now, shift your focus back to your body. Still with your eyes closed, notice that a column of white light is descending from high above you. It's moving slowly down towards your body. Down, down, until you feel it enter your energy body, then your physical body, down through your crown chakra, descending past your third eye and moving down, through your throat, your heart, your solar plexus, and your sacrum and into your root chakra. There the light pauses and pulsates, filling your whole being and body with an incredible surge of energy.

You are like a finely tuned race car revving its engine, the motor surging in tiny anticipatory increments as the car makes its way toward the starting line.

The energy of the light within you is barely contained. It continues filling your entire being until you think you might burst. Then it blasts down and out through your root chakra into the Earth, moving rapidly down, down, down until it reaches the core of the planet and is anchored.

Once you are anchored, you are connected to the Divine and to the planet that sustains you. This may be a more powerful grounding experience than you have yet experienced. You are firmly and solidly anchored in the love of your Creator and sustained by Mother Earth. Rest here for a moment, before continuing. Breathe.

From the empowered place you have reached, you are ready to set out anew upon your soul journey. Bright vistas await you. Your being has been reprogrammed by this meditation. Your soul settings have been returned to default, to the most perfect attunement for you.

As you sit, embodying this beam of light, you are wrapped in the loving arms of the Universe. You are nurtured and cared for more than you can imagine. You are a magnificent, beautiful soul, resplendent in your brilliance. Now do you see your true self? Do you recognize the truth of who you are? Soak it in. Memorize it. As you sit and breathe, allow the light to fill your heart and your mind, and to erase any remaining darkness or doubts you may be holding on to about your magnificence.

Should you find yourself reverting to old, destructive patterns later, you can revisit this place in another meditation. Just repeat the same steps. You can always reconnect, reset, and move forward refreshed, sure of yourself and your place in the Universe. No one can take this away from you.

When you are ready to end the meditation, focus again on your breathing and slowly start to shift your focus externally to the room you are seated in and your third-dimensional surroundings. Take your time, there's no hurry. When you feel ready, open your eyes.

Sit quietly for a few moments, allowing the massive energetic shift to reverberate through your awareness and understanding. Allow yourself to become fully present, perhaps standing up and stretching a little to reconnect with your body. Move slowly and deliberately as you reorient yourself. Then feel free to go about your day.

This meditation has been a gift from your Akashic team. They know what you are capable of, and await the day when at last you do too. They want you to know:

Together we are unstoppable, and so shall it be from now until eternity. Go in peace, precious child.

After the Meditation

I highly recommend that you drink some water to rehydrate.

I also encourage you to make some notes. Write down your feelings and observations about this experience. Being able to refer to your notes will be important later if challenges arise that cause you to doubt yourself.

Go easy on yourself for the next hour or so. Then as you return to your routines, look at them with fresh eyes. Listen for inspiration about changes that you can make. Go slowly. There's no rush. You don't want to burst out and over correct what you've been doing. Take baby steps. Slow and steady progress will serve you well.

At least once a week (more is better), write in your journal. Record new thoughts, ideas, inspiration, observations. Having multiple entries to compare will help on those days when you feel challenged and need to have evidence of your progress.

In one month, review the entirety of what you have written. Use the review to observe your life with new eyes. If you're like other people who have used this meditation, you will perceive that you are not the same person you were a month ago. You will have new clarity, new insights, and new inspiration.

It would be wise to continue this practice beyond the month, but that is up to you.

MESSAGE TO HUMANITY

As I was putting the final touches on this book, my Akashic guides sent this special message to pass along to you.

The human race is dangling on a precipice. People may choose to right the ship, or they may choose to tumble over the edge into oblivion.

Do not be alarmed. Should every human on the Earth be extinguished, more would come forth aided by neighbors in the galaxy. Annihilation of this generation would most certainly upset the plans many have for their current incarnations, but it definitely would not be the end of humans on

Earth. They go together like a horse and carriage.

The wiser choice for humankind, of course, would be to draw back from the precipice. To find ways to work together. To create more harmony among the diverse peoples of the planet.

In order to take that fateful leap off the precipice, all souls would have to agree. Remember your free choice? So long as there is hope, we do not expect that annihilation of the world will be the case, so take heart. There is still time to change. There is still time to finish this incarnation and begin another. Time is infinite.

We only want you to see that bringing the people of the planet together into a co-operative effort will benefit all. What can you do today to spread harmony among your fellow beings? It really does not require much of a shift. Merely a small adjustment in intention and you would start a wave rippling across the planet that would act like a beacon calling others to the cause.

It's what they have been waiting for. A sign, an honest to goodness concrete sign that they can hold onto and believe in.

They have not yet come to understand that they need not rely upon outer signs. They have everything they need within their very own soul. They only need come to a place of understanding and apprecia-tion for their own divinity. When they at last understand, they will be unstoppable. They will unleash their soul's potential and become part of the glorious solution.

That is one possible future. We hope you will choose that path. We'll certainly be do-ing everything in our power to help you get there, and to take positive action to bring forward this version of your future.

We don't mind sharing that some days we are quite weary as we work on your be-half, while you seem incapable of helping yourselves. It is such anathema to who you are as souls. If only you could get out of your head more and follow your internal compass. So much disappointment could be avoided. You would progress more quickly towards the better feeling place.

Allow yourself to feel more, think less. We think that would be a fine mantra to share with your fellow planetary residents. Sing it out loud and clear for the whole world to pick up the rhythm and the beat. Allow the resonance to pollinate those souls and help them awaken to the truth of who and where they are.

As more and more children awaken, the resonance will grow stronger and it will attract more souls like bees to honey. That's the way to start a movement, and the ripple will spread out across the galaxy. That's what a little bit of intention and momentum can do.

ACKNOWLEDGMENTS

Special thank you to my publishing team. I am grateful to editor Stephanie Gunning, who took on the challenge of "molding me into an author," artist Gus Yoo, who created a cover that encapsulates my vision of the Akasha, book coach Vassia Sarri, who held my hand and encouraged me every step of the way, coaches (and friends) Donna Blevins, Jackie Simmons, Katya McKewen, and Reverend Anne Presuel, who said, "You must write a book."

Much appreciation to my Akashic Warriors. You answered the call and stepped up in the home stretch with your support and encouragement. You are my heroes.

Finally, love and gratitude to my entire family, spread far and wide. Thank you for the strong foundation upon which everything was built.

RESOURCES

Edgar Cayce's Association for Research and
Enlightenment: EdgarCayce.org

Parelli Natural Horsemanship:
Parelli.com

Abraham-Hicks:
Abraham-Hicks.com

Linda Howe: LindaHowe.com

Sacred Angel Numbers:
SacredScribesAngelNumbers.blogspot.com

ABOUT THE AUTHOR

Debbra Lupien, is an Author, Motivational Speaker, and Akashic Records Expert.

Her fervent belief is that the most important question in life is: *What feeds your soul?* When you answer that and start doing it, you'll be unstoppable. Who doesn't want that?

Learn more and get your reader bonuses at: AkashaUnleashed.com/treats.